Drafting

"This book will have you drawing professional-looking house plans before you know it—even if you can't tell a T-square from a pencil sharpener. . . ."

—*Practical Homeowner*

"A simple but effective guide to drafting."

—*Yankee Homes*

"The joy of Mr. Syvanen's books is [that] he makes everything seem easy."

—The *Berkshire Courier*

"Bob has an uncanny ability to explain procedures you just can't find explained anywhere else."

—*The Whole Earth Catalog*

NOV '94

WI

by Bob Syvanen

Drafting: Tips and Tricks on
Drawing and Designing House Plans

Carpentry and Exterior Finish: Some Tricks of the Trade

Carpentry and Interior Finish: More Tricks of the Trade

Getting a Good House:
Tips and Tricks for Evaluating New Construction

Drafting:
Tips and Tricks on Drawing and Designing House Plans

Second Edition

by Bob Syvanen

The Globe Pequot Press

Old Saybrook, Connecticut

Copyright © 1982, 1993 by Bob Syvanen

Library of Congress Cataloging-in-Publication Data

Syvanen, Bob.
    Drafting : tips and tricks on drawing and designing house plans /
by Bob Syvanen. -- 2nd ed.
        p.   cm. -- (Home builder's library : v. 1)
    ISBN 1-56440-250-9
    1. Architectural drawing--Technique. 2. Architecture, Domestic-
-Designs and plans. I. Title. II. Series.
    NA2708.S98   1993
    728'.37'0221--dc20   93-11223
                                                                CIP

Manufactured in the United States of America
Second Edition/First Printing

Contents

INTRODUCTION vi

Section 1: EQUIPMENT.............1
Drafting Boards 2
Triangles 6
Scales 7
Pencils 8
Sharpeners...............................9
Templates 11
Paper 13
Light Tables 13

Section 2: DESIGN.................15
Styles....................................16
Measuring Tools 19
Stairs 22
Chimneys 24
Halls & Closets 25
Location 26
Quick Topographical Survey 28
Structural Considerations..........29
First Sketches 35

Section 3: DRAFTING............39
Step 1 41
Step 2 42
Step 3 43
Step 4 44

Step 5....................................45
Step 6....................................47
Dimension Lines......................48
Step 7 51
Step 8 53
Step 9 54
Step 10 55
Roof Texture...........................56
Sidewall Texture 57
Step 11 59
Details...................................60
Section 61
Electrical 62
Plot Plan 63
Door & Window Schedule........64
Room Schedule 65
Lettering 66
Symbols & Abbreviations 69
Typical Floor Framing Plan.......71
Typical Roof Framing Plan 72
Typical Floor Plan 73
Rough Details..........................74
Large Scale Details...................77
Refined Details 81
Perspectives 82
Landscape Plan 84
Small House Plan 87
Small House Plan 95

Introduction

If you plan to build your own house, there is no better way to start than by drawing the plans. There is no way to succeed at a task without giving it a try. It's been said that most of us use about 5 percent of body-mind potential; so with a little effort, surely we can tap that other 95 percent. I have felt for some time now that anyone can do anything, and designing and drawing your own house plans is just another one of those things anyone can do.

With the high cost of everything, here is an area where a substantial saving can be made. A $100,000 house, designed and drawn by an architect, would cost from $2,400 on up, depending on design (complicated designs cost more). If a draftsman draws the plans, they would cost from $1,200 on up. Many architects won't touch the small house plan. Plans for a $200,000 house, architect designed and drawn, would cost from $4,800 on up; draftsman drawn, $2,400 on up. The bottom line is a saving of at least 50 percent when plans are drawn by a draftsman, a good inducement for the home builder to use one. Even better, there is a 100 percent savings when you do the drafting. An added bonus is the ability to say, "I did it myself."

Most problems are or should be ironed out on paper before the first stick is cut; it's cheaper that way. The more knowledge you have on the total subject, the better the end product will be. In fact, I got into carpentry forty years ago so that I would be a better architect. My carpentry books would be a help in both designing and building. I always keep the carpenter in mind when I design a house, but my primary interest is the client's ideas. I try to put on paper what the client wants, not what I want. I merely suggest and guide. You, as designer, can do the same with that inner wisdom we all have. Very few houses that are built are architect designed; so come on in, the water's fine!

Section 1: Equipment

You can draw the same set of plans with a T square, two wood pencils, a kitchen table, and a triangle as you can with a fancy table, seven triangles, and five pencils. One set will cost $15, the other $2,500; but it all boils down to hand and head.

The bare-bones equipment and desire are all you really need for drawing your own house plans.

A table with a straightedge will work fine for a drafting board.

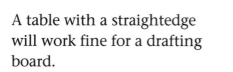

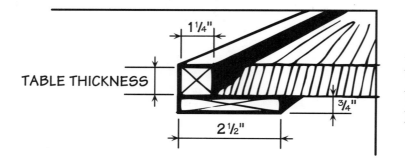

TABLE THICKNESS

1¼"

2½"

¾"

Any table will work fine, even one without a straightedge. Just make one up from two pieces of wood. Straight pieces would help.

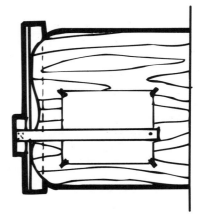

Clamp it to the end of the table.

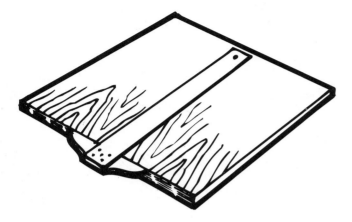

You can buy a small board for about $25.

Or you can make one from ¾-inch AC plywood, bought or scrounged. If a T square is to be used, one end has to be straight and smooth. To get a nice slick end, cement a piece of formica (kitchen countertop material) to the edge (it is too hard to use for the surface). A sheet of hard surface paper or vinyl (available at drafting supply stores for $28 a square yard) makes a nice work surface. Vinyl is soft enough so that pencil work won't tear even thin tracing paper. It's easy to clean and lasts forever. Attach it to the board with 1-inch double-coated tape.

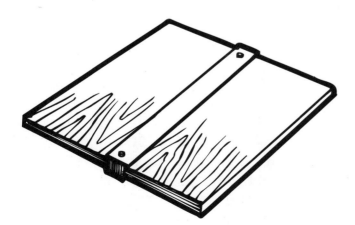

There is a nice little 18-by-24-inch board with a parallel straightedge for about $60. The largest one I know of is 23 by 31 inches and the smallest is 12 by 17 inches.

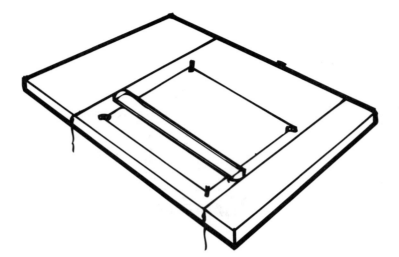

Parallel straightedges come in sizes 36, 48, 54, 60, and 72 inches. I like the 48-inch size, a nice in-between length. You don't have to hold a straightedge and triangle as you would a T square. It is always parallel no matter where you push it on the board. Be sure the board is longer than the straightedge.

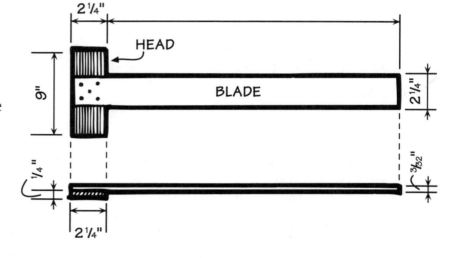

Since the parallel straightedge was refined, the T square isn't used much these days. But you can do good work with it. If you make one, try to make the blade perpendicular to the head, but don't be concerned if it is not; it will still slide up and down parallel. Just be sure the blade is straight and smooth and firmly anchored to the head with five wood screws.

A solid-core door makes a beautiful table (very heavy, but a nice surface). There are plenty of used doors at building salvage yards. A hollow-core door will do if you choose carefully. The older hollow-core doors have a better surface than the new ones. The smoother the surface the fewer problems you will have in keeping the drawings clean. The little bumps get rubbed by the tools, smudging the drawing. Doors for tops will be about 3 feet by 7 feet. I wouldn't go over 2 feet by 3 feet with ¾-inch plywood unless it is reinforced underneath to prevent sag and warp. Sand the surface and brush it clean before putting paper or vinyl on. Any small particles will cause bumps on the surface.

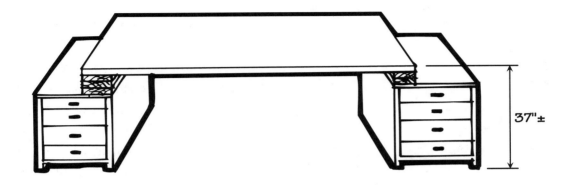

The height of the board is a matter of personal preference; remember you might want to work both sitting and standing. My board is 37 inches high and flat; I don't like to chase pencils. Most people like the board raised a few inches on the far edge. If the board is high (37 inches), then you must sit on a high stool, 30 inches in my case. Table height (29 inches) is fine to work at only if you are sitting. The board can be supported on horses made for the job or blocked up on cabinets, dressers, or boxes.

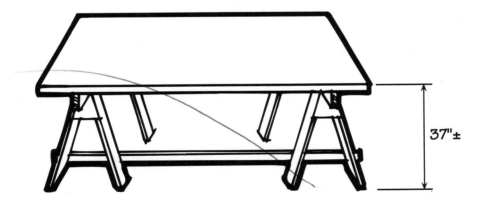

If plywood is used, a wood subframe should be built
and the whole business supported.

Any triangle will do the job if it is as long as the longest vertical dimension line on the plan. The bigger the board, the bigger the triangles can be. My first triangle was a 6-inch wood one, and I now use an 18-inch 30°-60° and a 12-inch 45°. The ones I find equally useful now are the 10-inch triangles.

A really great triangle is the 10-inch adjustable that comes in two styles. One measures degrees; the other, roof pitches. Either will do, but since my roof-pitch one vanished I cannot locate another—a good reason to scratch your initials on tools!

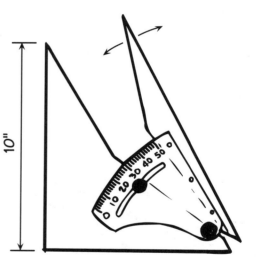

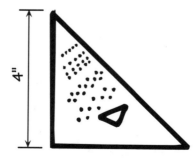

Another good triangle is the 45° lettering guide. There is a 6-inch model, but I find the 4-inch K&E 1895-C-4 model good enough.

The Ames lettering guide is probably the most common guide around, but take your pick.

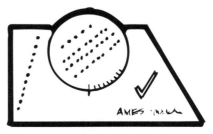

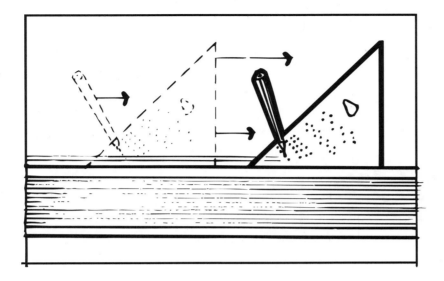

It is pretty obvious how the lettering guides are used—the pencil point is put into a hole of your choice and then you slide the triangle along the straightedge with the pencil. Bring the whole business back, put the point in a hole that will give the spacing desired, and then slide again. Presto, two parallel lines! One caution: The guides get dirty. Keep them clean and use only for lettering work or else you will find the drawing will get messy.

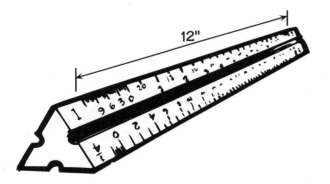

House plans don't have to be drawn super accurately as long as the numbers are correct. I used a plain wooden ruler with 1/16-inch increments when I started. The 12-inch triangular scale is the most familiar, and an inexpensive wooden scale will measure the same as an expensive one but will be harder on the eyes.

This 6-inch flat scale has eight scale graduations, four on the top and four on the bottom.

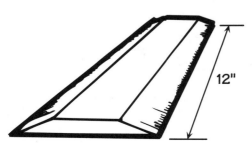

This flat scale has four scale graduations, and they are all visible on the top. The triangular scales always seem to have the scale you need on the bottom.

In the early days everything was inked after first drawing in pencil. What a drag! Now all we need is good pencil work, and wood pencils work fine.

Use any sharp tool to cut away the wood, leaving about ¾ inch of lead exposed.

The lead is then sharpened by rubbing the tip on a piece of sandpaper. Wipe the dust off when finished.

The mechanical pencil saves a lot of time. The one most used is a pencil-shaped metal tube with a chuck at the point end that holds one long piece of lead. The lead is advanced by pressing the rear of the pencil with the thumb, opening the chuck. The lead is free to slide out as far as needed. To sharpen, the tip is inserted into a pencil sharpener or rubbed on a piece of sandpaper. I use this style pencil with an H or F lead for heavy line work and heavy lettering.

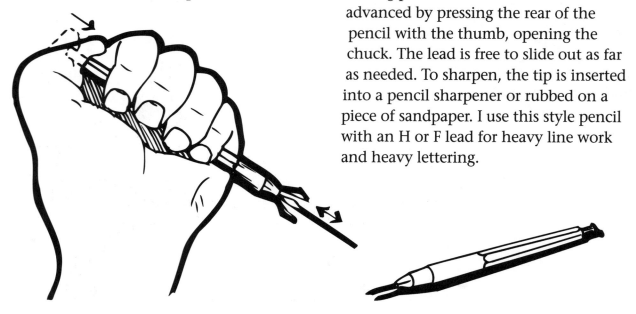

I think the best pencil to come down the pike is the 5-mm microlead. Not everyone can use this pencil without constantly breaking the leads. It must be held nearly vertical and with a good touch. The barrel is loaded with a dozen leads, and a click of the thumb will advance the lead, similar to a ball-point pen. It's clean and it's quick. You can't beat it for layout work where you need a light touch. The leads come in all the standard degrees. I find the 2H good for layout and the H or F good for lettering.

The microleads need no sharpening, all others need at least a piece of sandpaper. There is a 4-inch wood stick with a dozen pieces of sandpaper glued on made just for sharpening leads.

There is a neat little K&E sharpener. Might be hard to find, but there are similar ones.

Just insert the tip and twist.

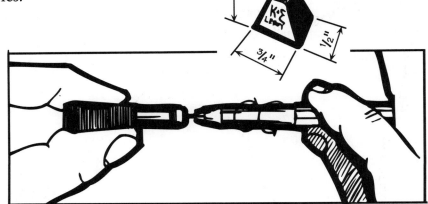

You can go to the bigger metal sharpeners.

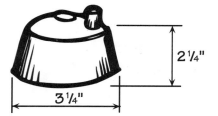

2 ¼"

3 ¼"

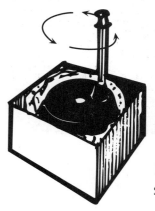

I keep the one I have in its box. Surround it with foam to keep it steady and to clean the point after sharpening.

KOH-I-NOR makes a nice plastic sharpener that clamps to the board.

RWS

All of these sharpeners create a lot of dust, so be careful. Wipe the lead points and brush off the drawing frequently, especially after erasing. Eraser particles are dirty and will smudge the drawing.

There is a 4-inch cloth bag, filled with clean ground-up eraser particles, that you pat on the drawing. This leaves salt-grain-size bits of eraser that the tools ride on.

A good way to keep drawings clean is to cover everything except the area being worked on. Any clean paper will do, but do tape it down. This is particularly good for a large drawing with much work on it.

A thin metal erasing shield is an inexpensive item worth having.

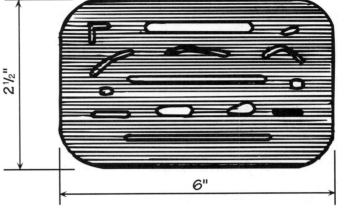

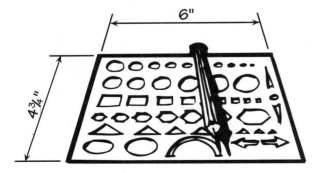

It lets you erase an area without disturbing what is around it. It also cleans the eraser.

There are three basic erasers: the vinyl, the gum, and the rubber. The old-fashioned "soap" or gum eraser is still a good one, but the vinyl is the most popular now. The "pink pearl" rubber eraser has been around a long time and it, too, is good.

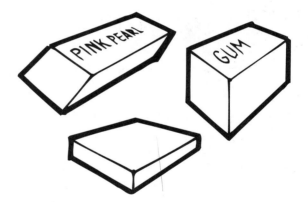

I have a couple of fancy compasses that I rarely use since acquiring circle templates. The one most used is a 4-by-6-inch combination circle, square, hex, triangle template. A good basic template. There is also a large circle template with radiuses from $\frac{1}{16}$ to 3 inches.

Plumbing-fixture templates, sometimes available from plumbing supply stores but more easily purchased at drafting supply stores, are handy tools. There are templates for just about anything you need to draw. They are very helpful but not necessary.

Three-quarter-inch-wide masking tape is a nice size to use for holding drawings on the board. Be sure to use drafting masking tape; it's not as sticky as the other tapes. You will have less trouble peeling it off. Scotch® tape No. 230 is a drafting masking tape.

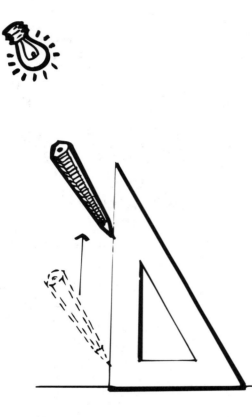

It is very important to have good lighting, and I am convinced that the best artificial light is full-spectrum lighting. I use two 48-inch Dura-test Vita-light fluorescents that have a color rendering index, CRI, of 91 (100 CRI for sunlight), and a color temperature of 5,500 degrees Kelvin. I also use a combination fluorescent-incandescent adjustable–clamp on desk lamp. It has a Dura-test full-spectrum 22-watt circine fluorescent and a Dura-test 75-watt neo-white incandescent. Any light should come from the upper left, for righties, upper right for lefties. Just be sure the straight edge or triangle does not cast a shadow on the line being drawn.

A right-handed person holds the triangle with the left hand and reaches across with the right to draw a vertical line.

A pocket calculator is a tool that is not necessary, but it sure helps me. It not only saves time and helps avoid errors, it makes math almost fun.

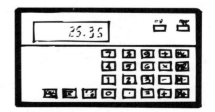

Tracing paper is pretty much a matter of preference. Any tracing paper will be fine, but some are better than others. For the serious draftsman I like clearprint 1000H, K&E Crystalene or K&E Albanene medium weight. All can be purchased by the roll or sheet. These papers have a "tooth" or texture that suits my hand and pencils. If photocopy is used for prints, then any kind of paper will do, but tracing paper is preferred for ease of tracing the different floor plans. If you have a light table, then anything goes.

I would not be without a roll of thin yellow tracing paper (the talking paper) and felt-tip pens. I find 14-inch and 18-inch wide by 50 yards the most useful and, at $5.00 a roll, well worth it. The choice of felt tip depends on what works best for you. Some people like working with fine lines, while others prefer heavy lines.

A light table can be very expensive, or you can make a wood-frame box with a few light sockets inside and a piece of ³⁄₁₆-inch or ¼-inch frosted glass for a work surface. A piece of ¼-inch plate glass on a couple of books at each corner and a light directed under is an effective light table. There is a lot of heat generated, particularly if the lights are enclosed, so ventilate.

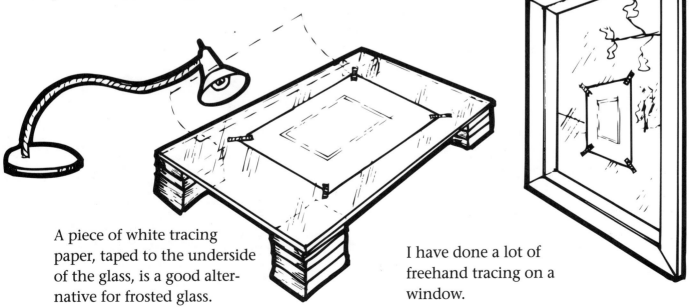

A piece of white tracing paper, taped to the underside of the glass, is a good alternative for frosted glass.

I have done a lot of freehand tracing on a window.

Equipment

Clean all triangles, straightedges, scales, templates, and tabletops before they get too dirty. It will go a long way towards keeping drawings clean. Clean drawings reproduce sharper and therefore are easier to read.

These are some basic tools. The drafting board is a 24-by-30-by-¾-inch piece of pine-faced plywood covered with vinyl. The surface under the vinyl should be smooth or every bump will show.

A few more tools to make the work easier.

The next step up. This board is a solid-core door, 3 feet by 6 feet, 8 inches. The vinyl covering over the birch door makes a nice smooth surface.

Section 2: Design

Most houses are owner or builder designed; so if you are an owner or builder, you can design your house. We all know a good house when we see it. We also know our limitations, or do we or others set our limits?

Keep in mind what the "experts" are stressing in light of the high cost of construction and fuel:

1. More energy-efficient construction.

2. Fewer and smaller bedrooms.

3. Fewer formal living rooms.

4. Summer and winter living (close off part of the house to conserve fuel).

5. Two generations under one roof.

The design information that follows is not very sophisticated, just very basic considerations, things like feelings, observation, stairways, chimneys, and so on. You can expand from these basics as your needs and desires dictate.

The first consideration in designing your house is to realize that you can do it. After all, you design every day when dressing . . .

. . . or arranging furniture, flowers, and drapes.

You look at a house and something clicks—it's good looking or it's awful. The roof angle is wrong; the chimney is too thin. Talk to yourself, call on that inner wisdom we all have. Take plenty of notes.

DON'T YOU THINK THE PIANO WOULD LOOK BETTER IN THE OTHER CORNER, MARY?

Next, consider your needs, wants, and life style. To start small because pocketbook and needs are small and add as they change is a good way to go. What we thought today frequently changes tomorrow.

ADD ANOTHER ROOM JOE, THE RABBIT DIED.

No matter what you design, half the people will love it and the other half hate it.

If you see a house you like, don't be afraid to copy it or use parts in your own design. All early caves were pretty much alike.

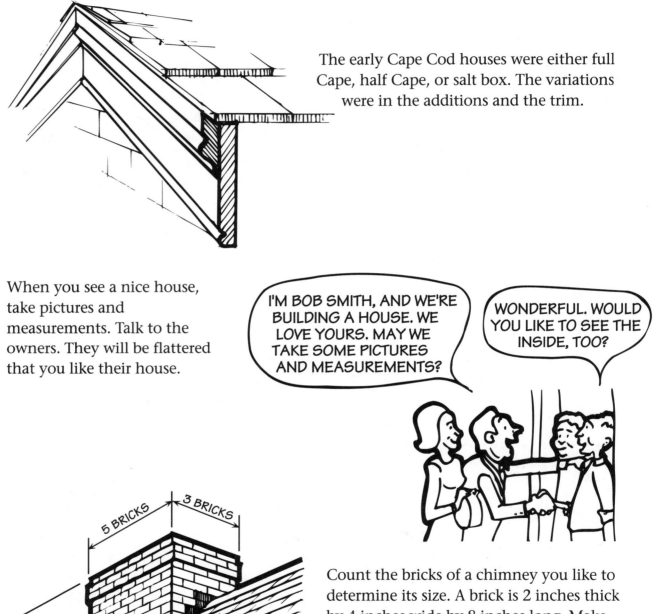

The early Cape Cod houses were either full Cape, half Cape, or salt box. The variations were in the additions and the trim.

When you see a nice house, take pictures and measurements. Talk to the owners. They will be flattered that you like their house.

I'M BOB SMITH, AND WE'RE BUILDING A HOUSE. WE LOVE YOURS. MAY WE TAKE SOME PICTURES AND MEASUREMENTS?

WONDERFUL. WOULD YOU LIKE TO SEE THE INSIDE, TOO?

Count the bricks of a chimney you like to determine its size. A brick is 2 inches thick by 4 inches wide by 8 inches long. Make note of the roof size and pitch. That same chimney might not look good on a different roof.

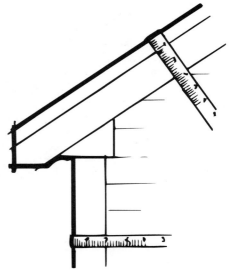

Carry a tape measure and pocket calculator. . . .

You might see a piece of trim you like. Or maybe it would look better thinner. Take notes; you will fill a book before you know it.

If you don't have a tape measure with you, use what you do have: your body. Know your stride (about 36 inches). . . .

3'-6"

A potential basketball star gets to count fewer steps.

2'-6"

Big doesn't always mean a long stride.

3'-0"

Some women have very long legs.

3'-0" ?

Don't stretch it; the stride will be inconsistent.

Plumbing vents look bad on the entrance side of the roof.

You never know when your tape will come in handy.

Think of the future.

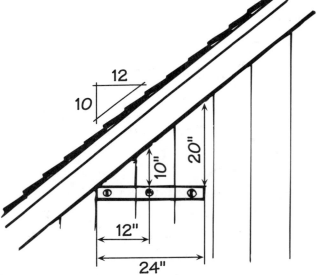

Use a carpenter's level and a tape measure to find the roof pitch.

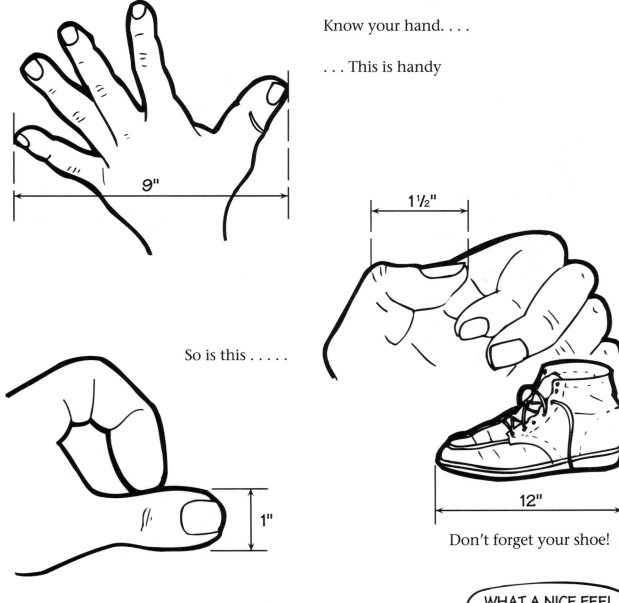

Know your hand. . . .

. . . This is handy

9"

So is this . . . . .

1½"

1"

12"

Don't forget your shoe!

WHAT A NICE FEEL TO THIS ROOM.

When in a room that feels good and comfortable, try to figure why. Is it the ceiling height, length-to-width ratio of the room, window sizes, and spaces? Measure all the contributing factors. How far is your raised hand from the ceiling? Count floor tiles; here is a good time to use your hand span. Tiles are either 9 inches or 12 inches. Take notes about things that don't please you, too; we learn from good and bad.

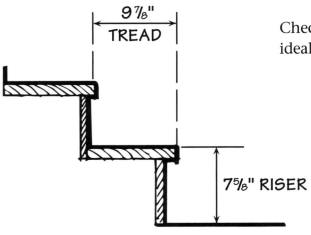

9⅞"
TREAD

7⅝" RISER

Check the rise and tread on stairs. There is an ideal or average, but are you average?

$$9\,⅞"$$
$$+\;7\,⅝"$$
$$\overline{17\,½"}$$

This is the ideal total of rise and tread.

Available space controls shape of stairways. . . .

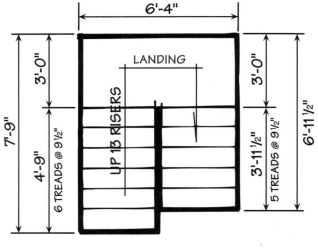

6'-4"

3'-0"

LANDING

7'-9"

UP 13 RISERS

4'-9"
6 TREADS @ 9½"

3'-0"

3'-11½"
5 TREADS @ 9½"

6'-11½"

PLAN

Code and comfort determine size.

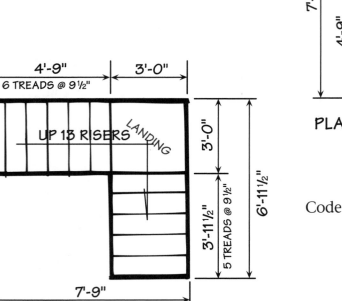

4'-9"
6 TREADS @ 9½"

3'-0"

UP 13 RISERS   LANDING

3'-0"

3'-11½"
5 TREADS @ 9½"

6'-11½"

7'-9"

PLAN

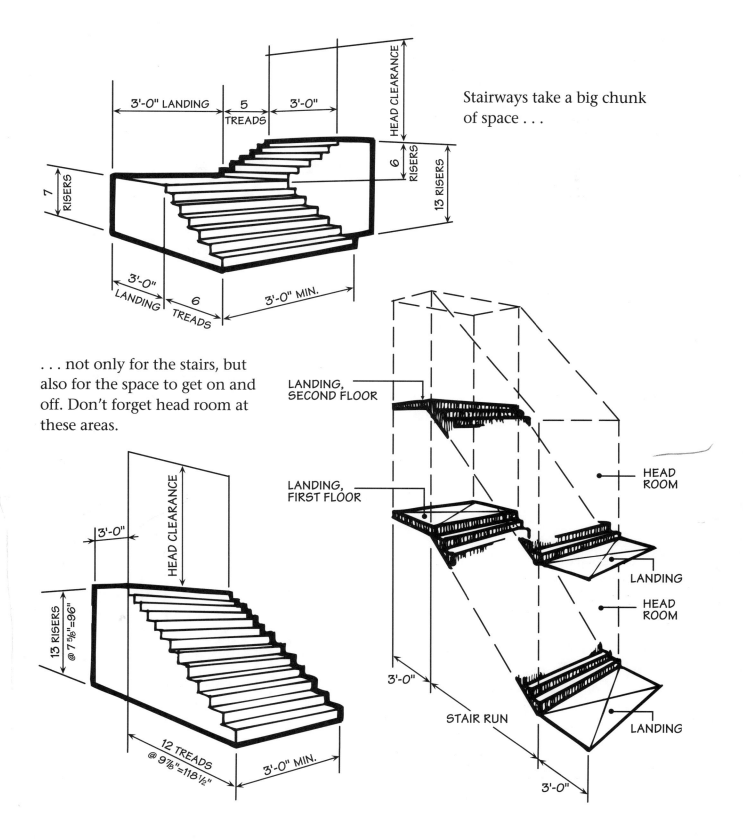

3'-0" LANDING • 5 TREADS • 3'-0"

HEAD CLEARANCE

7 RISERS

6 RISERS

13 RISERS

3'-0" LANDING • 6 TREADS • 3'-0" MIN.

Stairways take a big chunk of space . . .

. . . not only for the stairs, but also for the space to get on and off. Don't forget head room at these areas.

HEAD CLEARANCE

3'-0"

13 RISERS @ 7 5/8"=96"

12 TREADS @ 9 7/8"=118 1/2" • 3'-0" MIN.

LANDING, SECOND FLOOR

LANDING, FIRST FLOOR

HEAD ROOM

LANDING

HEAD ROOM

3'-0"

STAIR RUN

LANDING

3'-0"

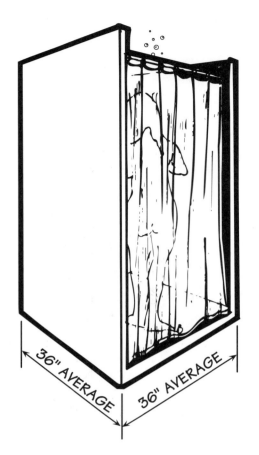

Bathrooms have spaces to consider—tub, sink, shower, john.

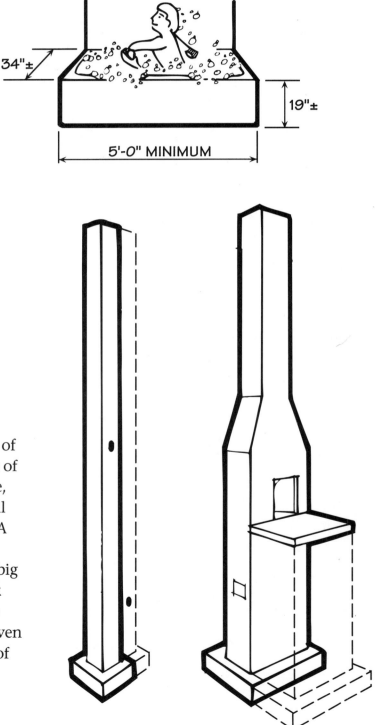

34"±

19"±

5'-0" MINIMUM

36" AVERAGE

36" AVERAGE

The fireplace takes another big chunk of space and is very central to the theme of the interior. When you see a good one, use it in your design, but be sure it will look good in the size room you plan. A big fireplace in a small room is overpowering, while a small one in a big room is lost. Remember the brickwork runs from basement to roof; the more flues it has, the bigger the chimney. Even a wood-stove chimney will take a lot of space from basement to roof.

The kitchen has the refrigerator, range, sink, and counter space as minimum requirements. Then there could be a wall oven, dish washer, broom closet, and table or counter. Take notes as you see layouts that are good and bad for you. You won't forget if you write it down.

3'-0" USUAL

Halls take a lot of space. They should be 3 feet wide for comfort, but they can be narrower if the local code will allow.

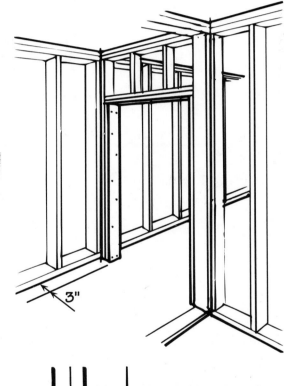

3"

A narrow hall makes for a narrow door at the end because of the framing required for the door. Making the trim thinner will require less framing material and then a wider door.

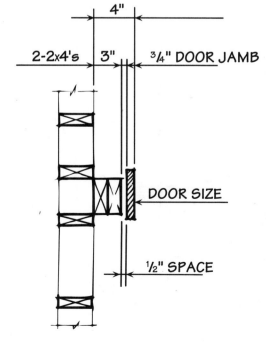

4"

2-2x4's | 3" | ¾" DOOR JAMB

DOOR SIZE

½" SPACE

A clothing closet should have a 2-foot depth for hanging garments.

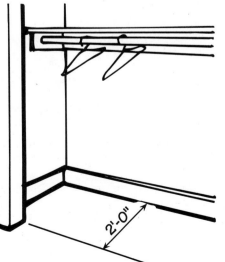

2'-0"

Other, and very important, considerations in design are: ground slope, sun, and trees. With the cost of fuel the energy-efficient house looks mighty good. We can at least take advantage of sun, shade, and wind buffers.

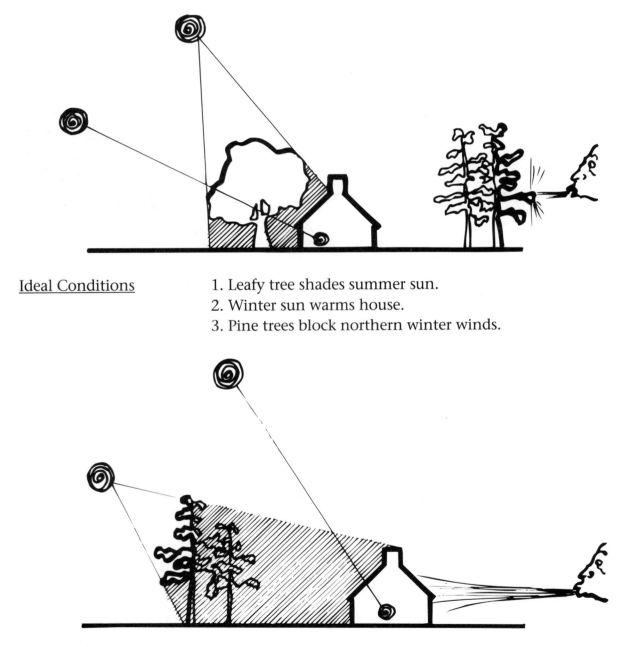

__Ideal Conditions__

1. Leafy tree shades summer sun.
2. Winter sun warms house.
3. Pine trees block northern winter winds.

__Bad Conditions__

1. Summer sun cooks house.
2. Pine trees block winter sun.
3. North winter winds chill house.

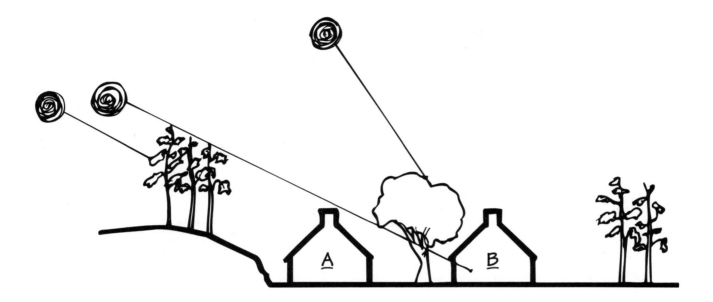

House B   Located better than house A.

House A   1. Pines block warming winter sun.
           2. Water run off from hill could cause damp basement.
           3. Summer sun cooks house.

House B   1. Leafy tree blocks summer sun.
           2. Winter sun warms house when leaves fall.
           3. Pine trees block north winter winds. Both houses benefit by this.

If the land slopes enough to the south and the winter sun is not blocked, then an underground house should be considered. Try to keep some leafy shade trees to block the summer sun.

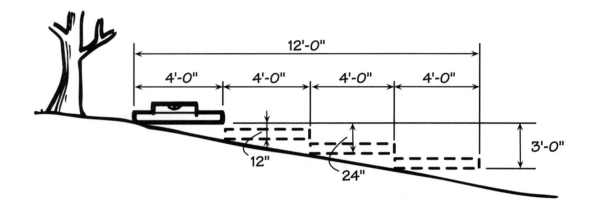

A good quick survey method for finding the slope of this ground is to use a simple carpenter's level, a few wood stakes, and a good eyeball.

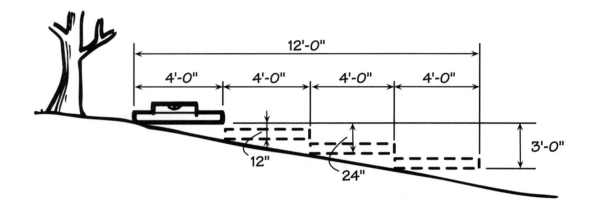

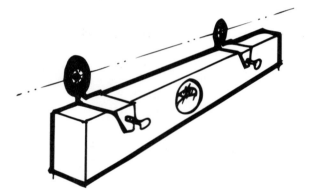

Stanley Tools makes an inexpensive set of level sights that clamp onto a wood carpenter's level. Good accuracy can be achieved with either system, certainly good enough to design with. If you can borrow a friend's builder's level (transit), so much the better, but it isn't necessary.

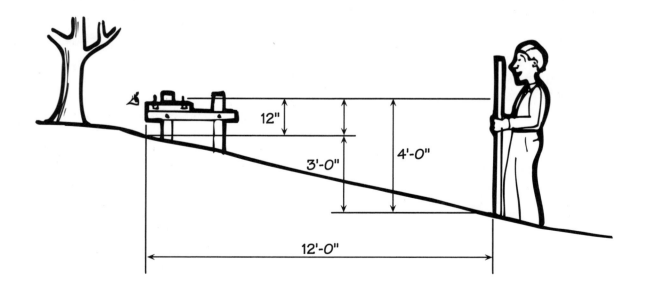

As for structural design, check the houses you visit. Go down to the basement and pace off the spans of the floor joists and beams.

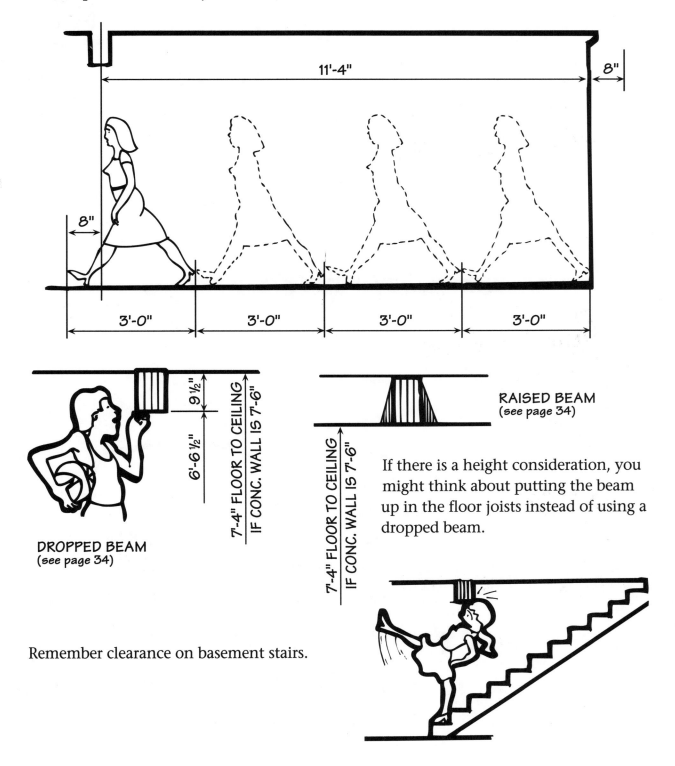

11'-4"   8"

8"

3'-0"   3'-0"   3'-0"   3'-0"

9½"

6'-6½"

7'-4" FLOOR TO CEILING IF CONC. WALL IS 7'-6"

DROPPED BEAM
(see page 34)

RAISED BEAM
(see page 34)

7'-4" FLOOR TO CEILING IF CONC. WALL IS 7'-6"

If there is a height consideration, you might think about putting the beam up in the floor joists instead of using a dropped beam.

Remember clearance on basement stairs.

Count the joists for spacing. Look in the attic for rafter sizes and spacing. Check a sagging roof, too; it tells you what not to do. If the dishes rattle when you walk across the floor, that tells you something, too. Check new construction.

HMM . . .
2x10 JOISTS AT 16" ON CENTER WITH SIX SPACES BETWEEN POSTS MEANS 8'-0" SPAN. BEAMS ARE FOUR 2x10's, AND IT FEELS SOLID UPSTAIRS; I'LL USE THE SAME STUFF IN MY NEW HOUSE.

Use the code books; they will tell you the size and spans for various framing conditions.

TABLE 1 MAXIMUM SPANS FOR GIRDERS	
SIZE	1 STORY
4x6	6'-0"

TABLE 2 MAXIMUM SPANS FOR FLOOR JOISTS		
SIZE	NO 1.	NO 2.
2x6	9'-1"	8'-6"

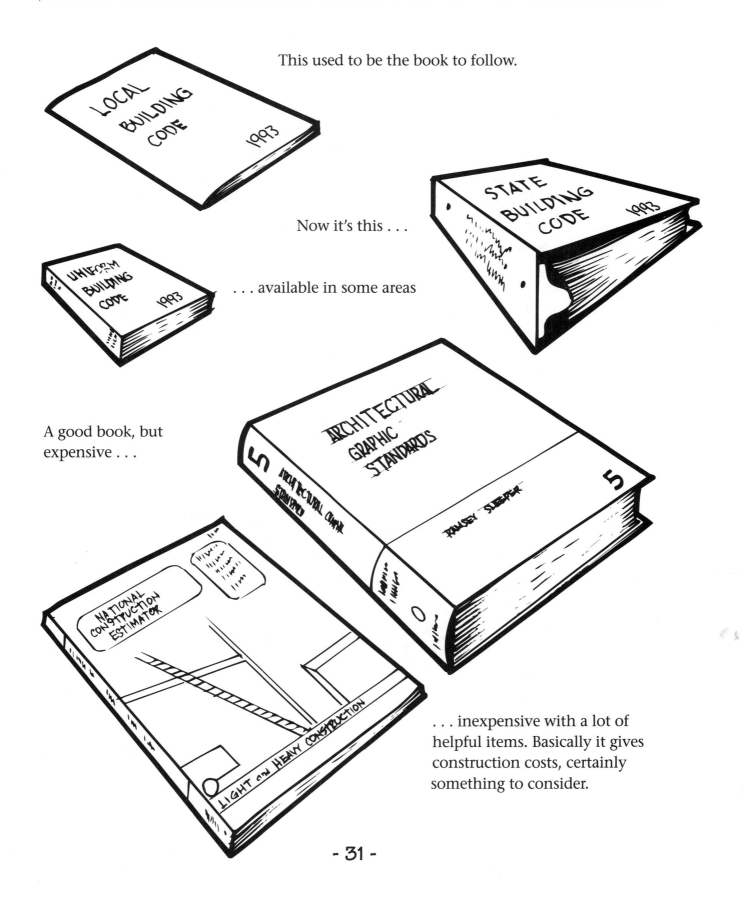

This used to be the book to follow.

LOCAL BUILDING CODE 1993

Now it's this . . .

STATE BUILDING CODE 1993

UNIFORM BUILDING CODE 1993

. . . available in some areas

A good book, but expensive . . .

ARCHITECTURAL GRAPHIC STANDARDS

5

RAMSEY SLEEPER

5

NATIONAL CONSTRUCTION ESTIMATOR

LIGHT AND HEAVY CONSTRUCTION

. . . inexpensive with a lot of helpful items. Basically it gives construction costs, certainly something to consider.

Any large department-store catalog has a wealth of information. Any item in house, garage, garden, or shop is covered by size, shape, color, and weight.

Local lumber yards sometimes have free or inexpensive design catalogs.

WILL A 4x10 BEAM WORK HERE?

Check with the building inspector; he is there to help you. Don't try to slip anything by him: he has ways of making up for it ten times over. One other caution: check with builders or carpenters about the inspector's ability to deal with the opposite sex, be it male or female. I have run across some male inspectors that give women a hard time. Don't fight him; try using a male friend to deal through. Of course follow the codes.

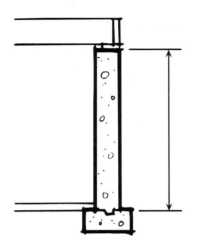

Foundation-wall heights are pretty much controlled by the local concrete contractor. His forms are just so high, limiting the height of the concrete pour. In my area, 7 feet, 6 inches is the common pour, but any height can be poured if the forms are modified. It always costs more if you stray from the normal conditions.

First- and second-floor minimum ceiling heights are sometimes set by code, and if not, use your own feelings. Try to keep stud lengths under 8 feet for economy.

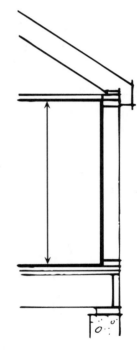

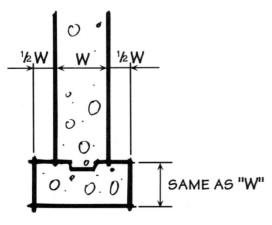

Concrete-wall thickness is generally set by code, and the footings are taken off that dimension.

The balloon frame is ideal for the energy-efficient house and worth considering when designing. Put 2x2 horizontal nailers on the studs, and you have the "Scandinavian wall." If you insulate between the studs, put a vapor barrier on the inside face and then the 2x2s, you will have an unbroken vapor barrier, a very important factor in insulating.

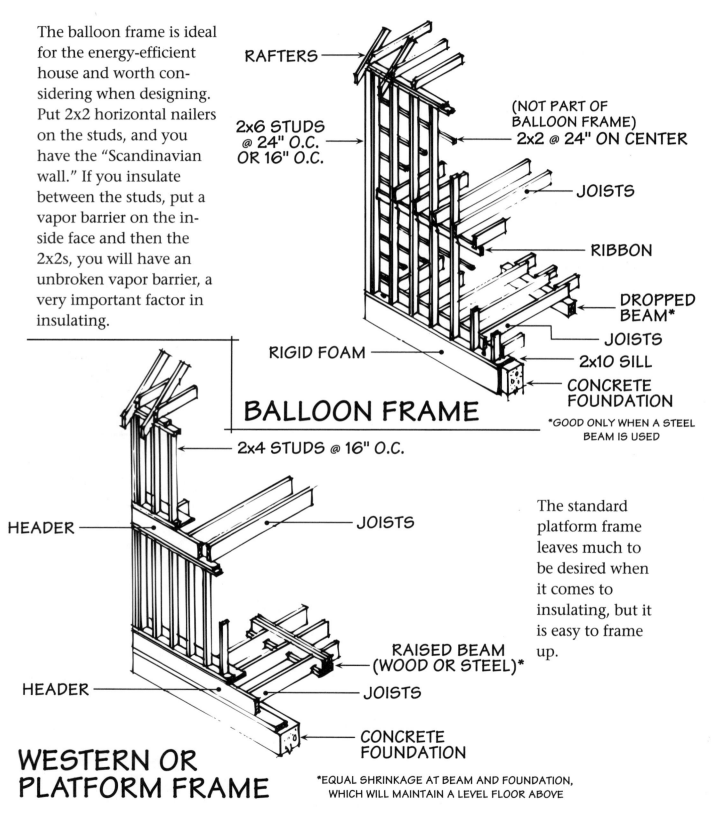

RAFTERS

2x6 STUDS @ 24" O.C. OR 16" O.C.

(NOT PART OF BALLOON FRAME) 2x2 @ 24" ON CENTER

JOISTS

RIBBON

DROPPED BEAM*

JOISTS

2x10 SILL

CONCRETE FOUNDATION

RIGID FOAM

BALLOON FRAME

*GOOD ONLY WHEN A STEEL BEAM IS USED

2x4 STUDS @ 16" O.C.

HEADER

JOISTS

HEADER

RAISED BEAM (WOOD OR STEEL)*

JOISTS

CONCRETE FOUNDATION

The standard platform frame leaves much to be desired when it comes to insulating, but it is easy to frame up.

WESTERN OR PLATFORM FRAME

*EQUAL SHRINKAGE AT BEAM AND FOUNDATION, WHICH WILL MAINTAIN A LEVEL FLOOR ABOVE

Once the basic house is decided on mentally, it is time to sketch. Use a felt-tip pen on yellow sketch paper (or any cheap paper). You might want to put a piece of graph paper under to help with the horizontal and vertical line work. Just let your inner wisdom go to town and check your notes. Use flat paper furniture cutouts, the same scale as the floor plans for room designing.

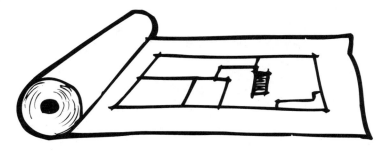

Keep an empty waste basket within "shooting" range.

When you make a good sketch but it needs a change, just lay the yellow tracing over and make a new sketch with the change. It is a fast way to work, and you will find your mind working fast, too.

This sketching is done for both the exterior and interior designs.

To firm it up, draw it freehand on graph paper. This will give you a better idea of sizes.

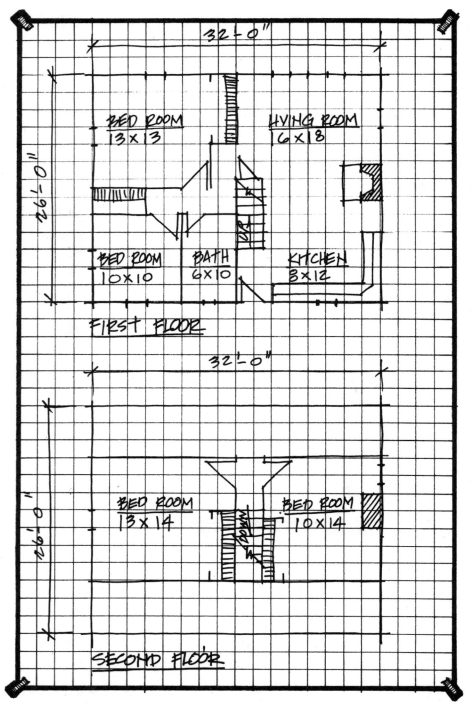

ONE SQUARE = 2 FEET

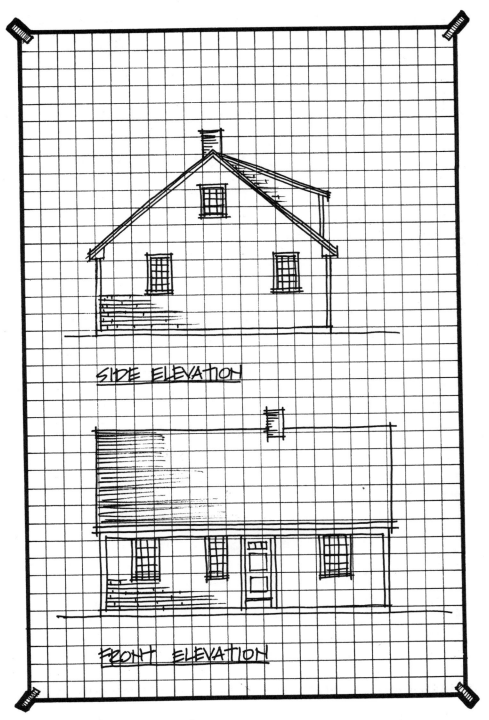

Do the same with the exterior.

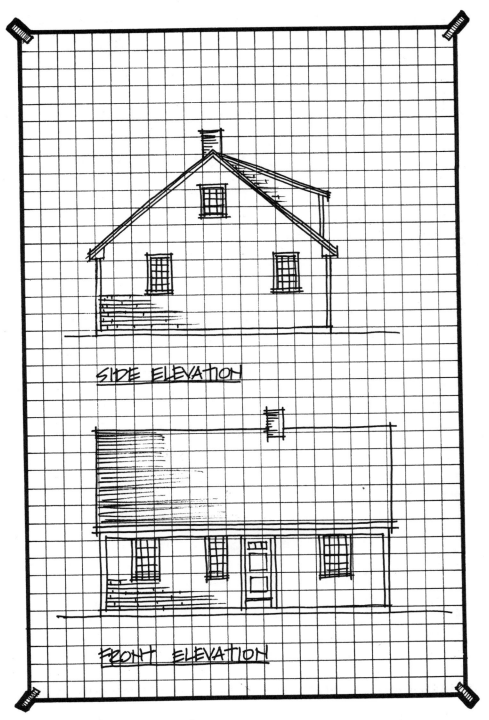

SIDE ELEVATION

FRONT ELEVATION

ONE SQUARE = 2 FEET

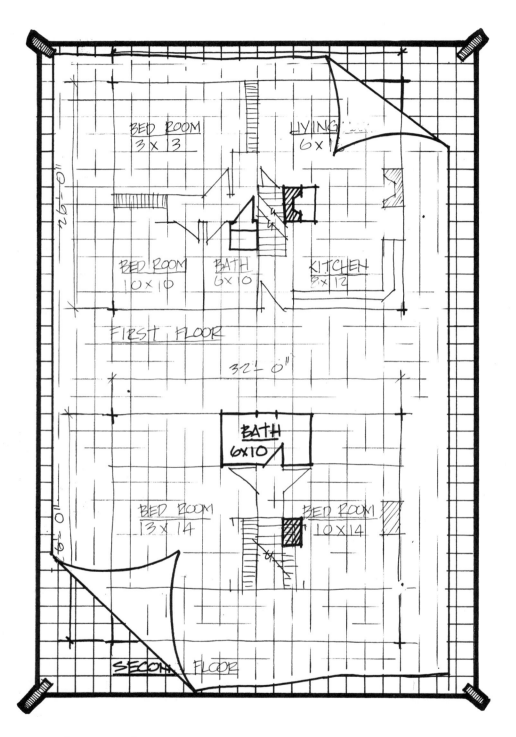

BED ROOM
3 x 13

LIVING
6 x

BED ROOM
10 x 10

BATH
6 x 10

KITCHEN
8 x 12

FIRST FLOOR

32'- 0"

BATH
6 x 10

BED ROOM
13 x 14

BED ROOM
10 x 14

SECOND FLOOR

If you want to make more changes, use the yellow tracing paper. You can work from the yellow tracing or back to the graph paper to start the working drawings. Remember, when using line sketches, that the wall thickness is not shown; keep that in mind when dimensioning.

Section 3: Drafting

You don't have to be a terrific artist to be a good draftsman. What it does take is observation and practice. Try to learn what makes for a good-looking job and then practice the techniques required. The plans don't have to be a fantastic work of art: as long as the builder knows what's going on, they will be fine. What can be difficult about running a pencil along a straightedge or measuring with a scale? With today's inexpensive calculators, mathematics becomes fun (almost). The only difficult thing is the lettering, and it is only difficult (at first) to make it stylish; anyone can make it legible.

⌑ Drafting

The first things to decide are what to draw on and what size the sheets will be. Because floor plans are traced one from the other, tracing paper would be a good choice. The sheet size is determined by the building size and the printing process. A 2-inch margin on each side and top with 3 inches on the bottom added to the length and width of the house will indicate the size sheet to use. The 2-inch and 3-inch margins allow space to write dimensions and titles. A house 26 by 32 feet drawn at ¼-inch scale will use a sheet 11½ by 12 inches. If the prints are to be photocopied, then the maximum-size sheet will be 11 by 17 inches (check with your local printer). The ½ inch lost on height can be fudged with the 3-inch bottom. The extra 5 inches can be used for details. Try to keep the details that are relative to the plan on the same sheet. If the prints are produced by the Ozalid process, then a much larger sheet can be used, but the 2-inch and 3-inch margins should be used in figuring the sheet size.

The number of sheets needed is determined by the sheet size and building inspector's requirements. A large sheet could have all the plans on one, a small sheet requires many sheets.

A good set of working drawings would be:

1. Foundation Plan ¼" = 1'-0"
2. Floor Plans ¼" = 1'-0"
3. Elevations ¼" = 1'-0" or ⅛" = 1'-0"
4. Section through Building ¾₈" = 1'-0" (shows construction)
5. Details 1½" = 1'-0"
6. Cabinet Elevations ¼" = 1'-0"
7. Fireplace Elevation ⅛₆" = 1'-0"
8. Floor Framing ⅛₆" = 1'-0"
9. Electrical Plan ¼" = 1'-0" (can be on floor plan)
10. Plot Plan 1" = 20'

Numbers one through four would be the minimum requirements.
Elevations can be at ⅛-inch scale to cut down on the number of sheets.

When the number of sheets is decided, cut them all at the same time or use precut sheets.

Determine sheet size and cut as many as needed.

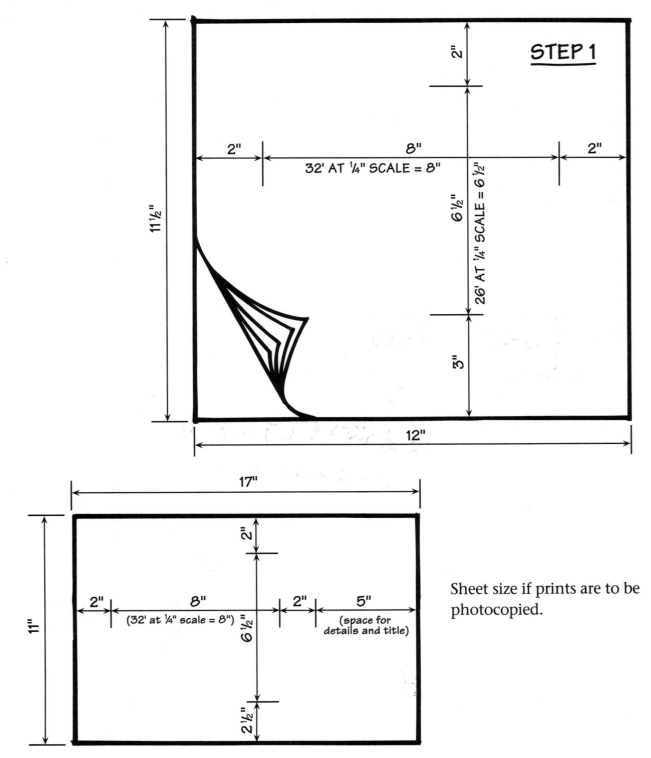

STEP 1

2"

2"   8"   2"
32' AT ¼" SCALE = 8"

11½"   6½"   26' AT ¼" SCALE = 6½"

3"

12"

17"

2"

2"   8"   2"   5"
(32' at ¼" scale = 8")   (space for details and title)

11   6½"

2½"

Sheet size if prints are to be photocopied.

⊜ Drafting

Tape the first sheet down and you are ready to lay out the first floor plan. Use a 2H lead with a light touch, just dark enough to see without too much trouble.

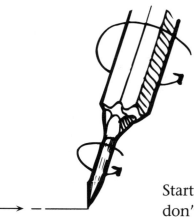

Always twirl the pencil with the fingers when drawing horizontal and vertical lines. This will keep the wear even on the point and the line will be a consistent thickness. It takes a little getting used to, but is a must.

Start with the perimeter of the house and then the partitions; don't worry about doors and windows yet. Draw the exterior walls 5 inches (at ¼-inch scale, close is good enough) if studs are to be 2x4 and 7 inches if 2x6. The interior partitions will be 2x4, so 4½ inches for them. These dimensions take into account the wall material, studs, siding, sheathing, and Sheetrock.

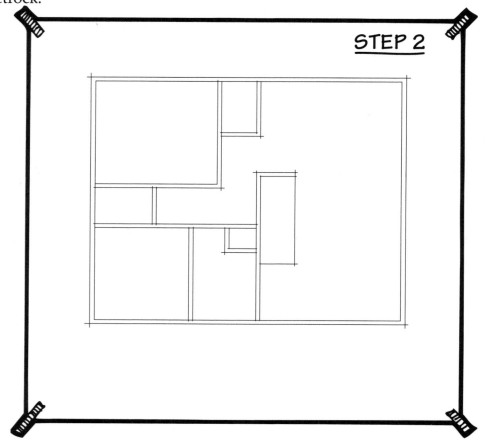

STEP 2

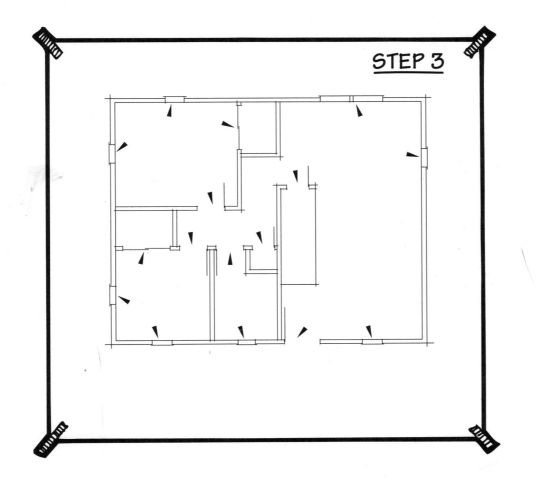

STEP 3

Locate doors and windows.

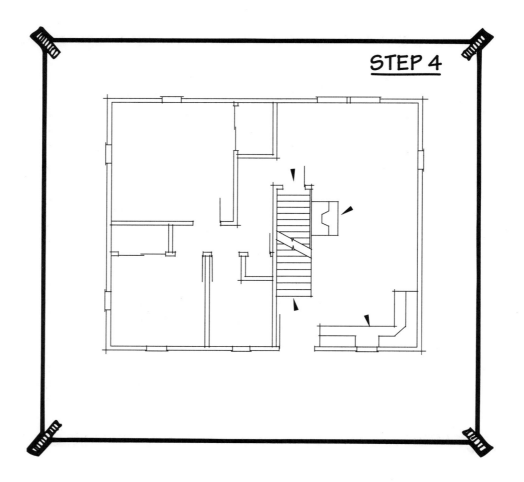

STEP 4

Locate stairs, fireplace, and kitchen cabinets.

Locate bathroom fixtures, kitchen sink, range, and refrigerator. When satisfied that all is well, darken the line work to make things clearer. Save the final punching up (dark and heavy line work) until after the dimensions are on. If line work is heavied up and work continues, the sheet will get dirty.

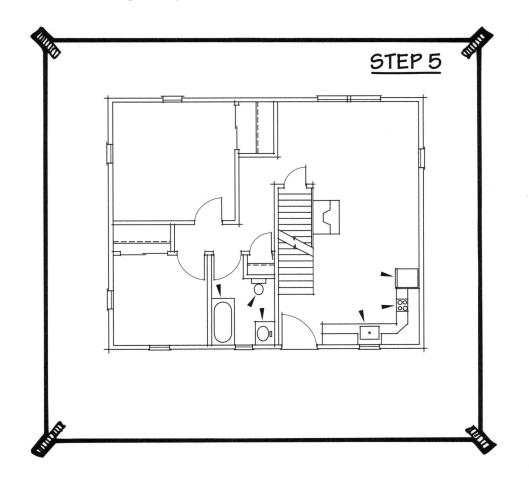

STEP 5

Where lines cross at corners, extend them past each other.

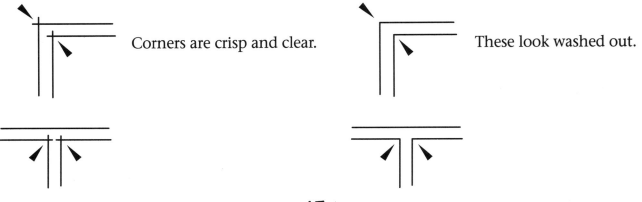

Corners are crisp and clear.   These look washed out.

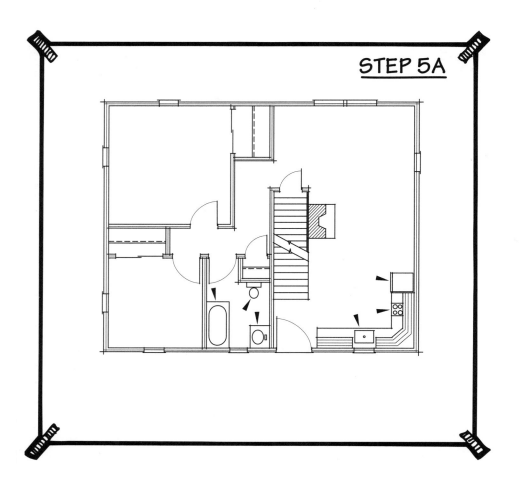

STEP 5A

Filling in the partitions with lighter parallel lines helps to show them up, although dimension lines won't be quite as clear. It is not necessary to do; it just dresses up the drawing.

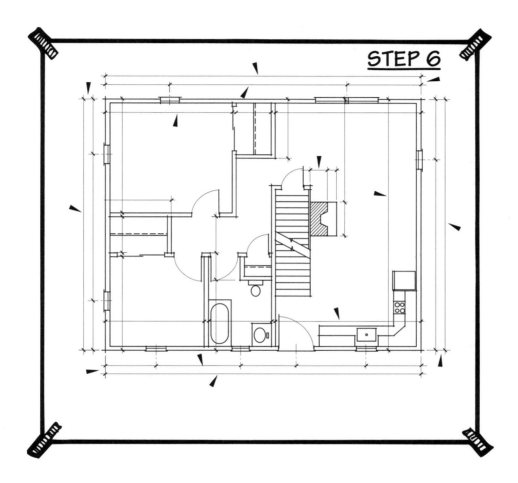

STEP 6

Dimension lines come next. They should be lighter than the partition lines but dark enough to be positive. The walls want to jump out at you.

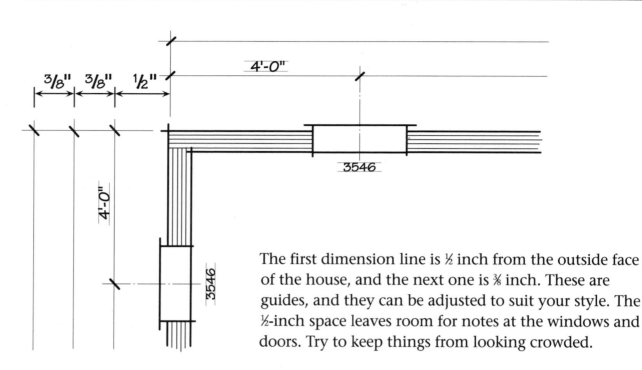

The first dimension line is ½ inch from the outside face of the house, and the next one is ⅜ inch. These are guides, and they can be adjusted to suit your style. The ½-inch space leaves room for notes at the windows and doors. Try to keep things from looking crowded.

There are three basic symbols for terminating dimension lines:

I favor this simple 45° freehand slash. It's easy and clear.

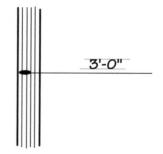

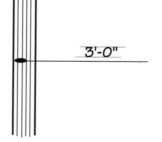

. . . simple, but not always clear as to where it ends.

Time-consuming to draw and not always clear as to where it ends . . .

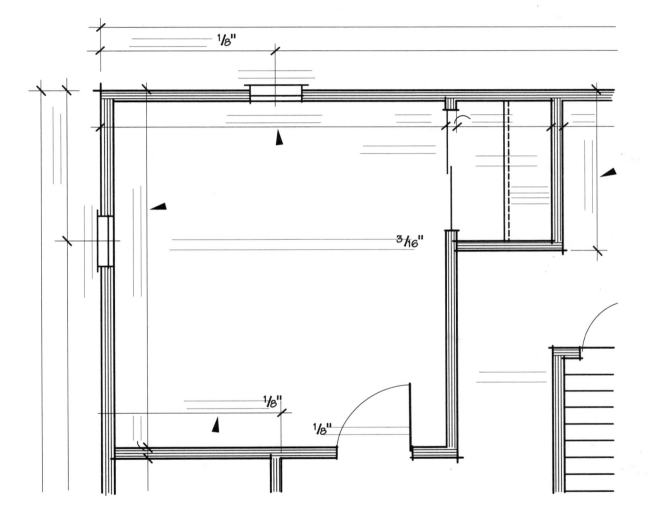

Inside dimension lines are kept near the walls to allow for room labeling and un-interrupted dimension numbers. The dimension number should be at the mid-point of what it is describing. Clarity is impaired if a dimension line runs through it. Sometimes it can't be helped. The dimension numbers of doors and windows are located on their center lines.

There are choices to be made when dimensioning inside partitions, and each has its good and bad points.

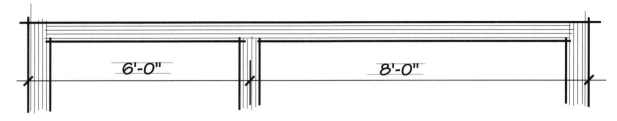

Using the center line of partitions is good, but make sure to be consistent. The carpenter then knows that he must locate each partition face off the center line on the plans.

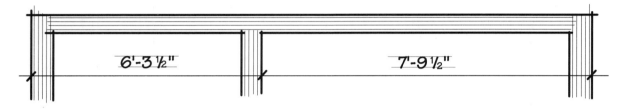

Dimension lines to one face of a partition (excluding the exterior, which is always to the outside face of stud) can be confusing. Many mistakes are made by putting the partition on the wrong side of the line.

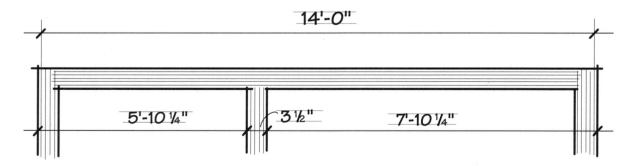

To dimension both sides of the partition is a lot more work for the draftsman but very nice for the carpenter. Most interior partitions are 3½-inch studs, which will cause quite a few fractions to come up in the dimensions; that is why some draftsmen use 4 inches for this dimension. The carpenter will then lay out the rooms using the 4 inches and adjust for the actual 3½-inch wall.

Whatever system is used, the sum of the inside dimensions must equal the exterior dimension; always check this out. Never use a dimension less than ⅛ inch anywhere; it's a house, not a piano. Stay with ¼-inch minimum for dimensions.

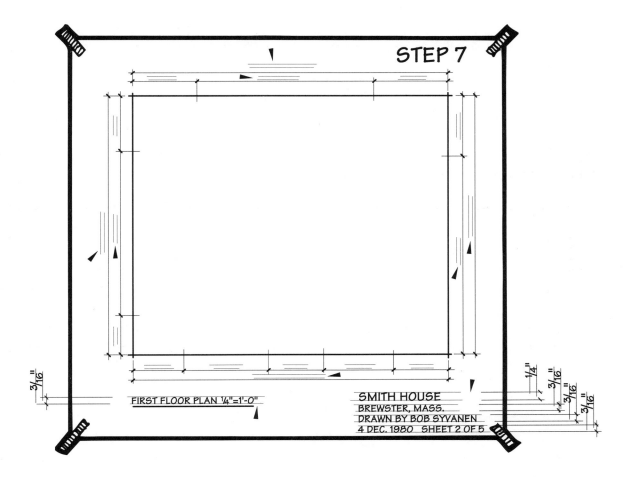

STEP 7

3/16"

1/4"
3/16"
3/16"
3/16"

FIRST FLOOR PLAN ¼"=1'-0"

SMITH HOUSE
BREWSTER, MASS.
DRAWN BY BOB SYVANEN
4 DEC. 1980   SHEET 2 OF 5

Put in all the lettering guidelines, and don't be afraid if they show up on the prints; I think they add to the look of the drawing. The sizes I use might not suit you; use them as a guide. Put the dimensions in after all the guidelines are in. Don't worry if the plan does not measure what the dimension reads unless it is very much out of scale. It's good if it is dimensioned as you want and the totals add up. I like to save all the large lettering for last and do all the sheets at the same time. The sheets stay cleaner, and the lettering is more consistent.

Vertical lettering is printed as
if the sheet is in this position.

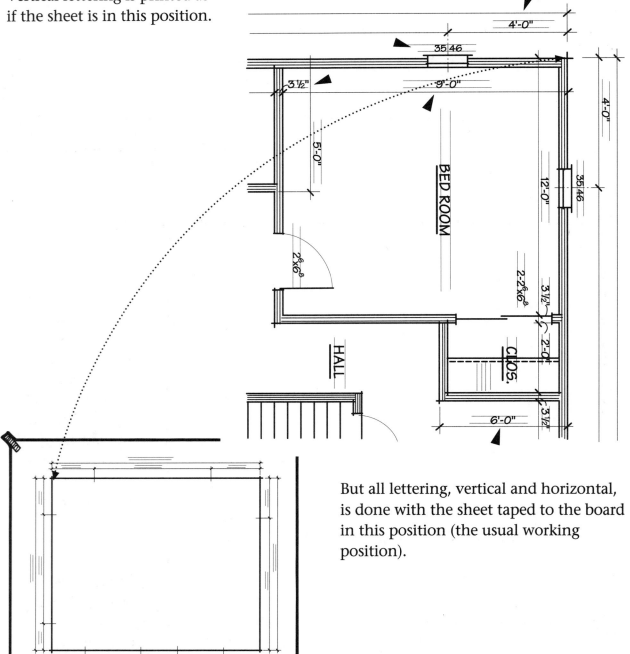

BED ROOM

HALL

CLOS.

4'-0"

35|46

3½"

9'-0"

5'-0"

4'-0"

12'-0"

35|46

2'-6^8

2-2'-6^8

3½"

2'-0"

2'-0"

3½"

6'-0"

FIRST FLOOR PLAN ¼"=1'-0"

SMITH HOUSE
BREWSTER, MASS.
DRAWN BY BOB SYVANEN
4 DEC. 1980 SHEET 2 OF 5

But all lettering, vertical and horizontal,
is done with the sheet taped to the board
in this position (the usual working
position).

The foundation plan is traced from the first floor plan.

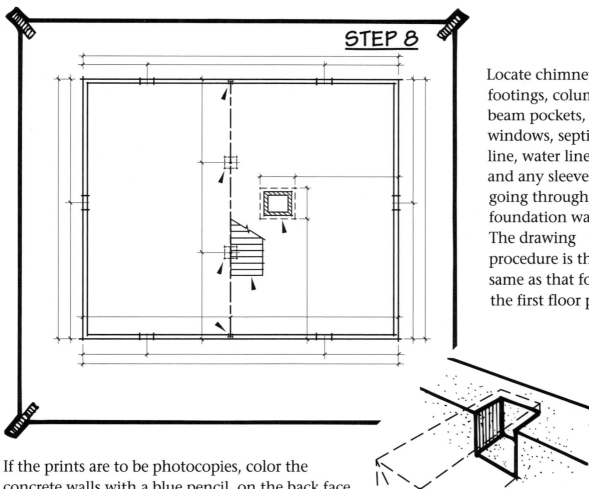

STEP 8

Locate chimney footings, columns, beam pockets, windows, septic line, water line, and any sleeves going through the foundation wall. The drawing procedure is the same as that for the first floor plan.

If the prints are to be photocopies, color the concrete walls with a blue pencil, on the back face of the drawings. Make it medium dark, and it will show a nice shading on the prints. Don't color the window openings.

BEAM POCKET

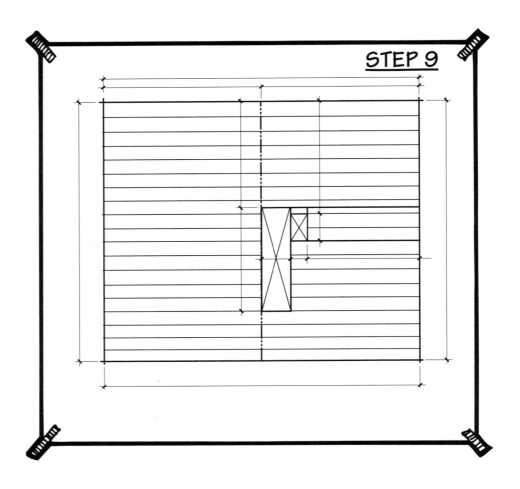

STEP 9

Lay another sheet over the foundation plan and lay out the floor framing plan. It is a good, safe way to draw the framing because the stairs, chimney, and floor beam are right there to see. A simple way to draw the joists is first to multiply the length by 12 inches to get the total inches. Then divide by 16 inches to get the number of joist spaces. The calculator does a great job here. Find a scale that is close enough to angle from one side to the other (see illustrations for siding spacing on page 58) and mark the spaces. Use single lines for all members, joists, headers, bridging, and blocking.

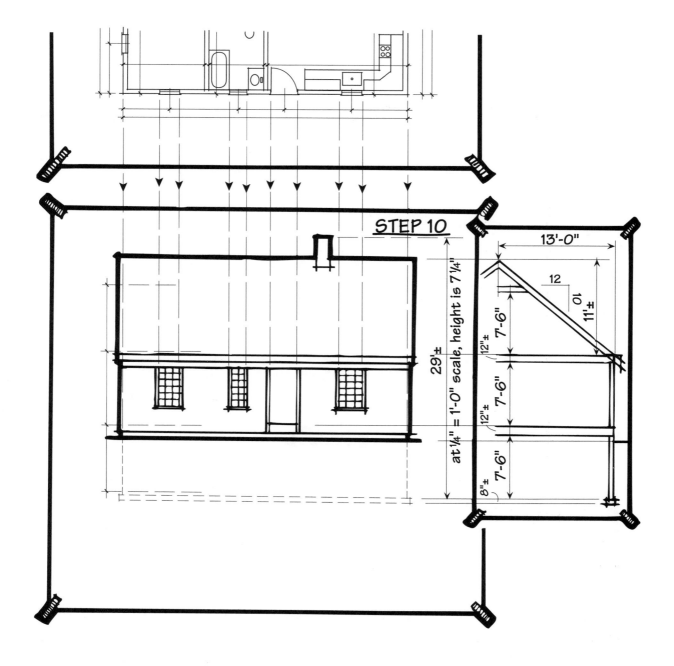

STEP 10

13'-0"

12

10

11'±

7'-6"

12"±

7'-6"

12"±

7'-6"

8"±

29'± at ¼" = 1'-0" scale, height is 7¼"

The elevations are projected off the floor plan and a ¼-inch scale section. If the elevations are drawn at ⅛-inch scale, everything must be measured off the ¼-inch scale plans or a photocopy reduction to ⅛-inch scale used.

Textures are drawn to suit your artistic sense. They should resemble the material used.

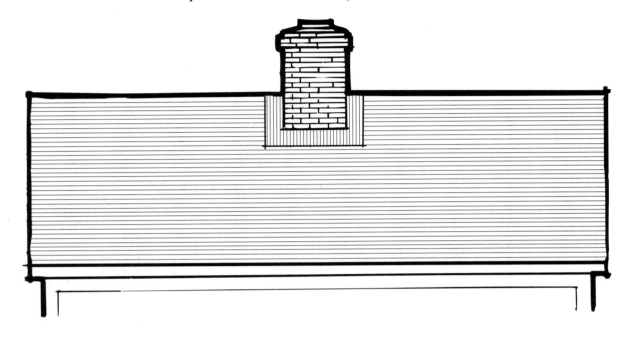

Roof with close parallel lines simulates shingle courses.

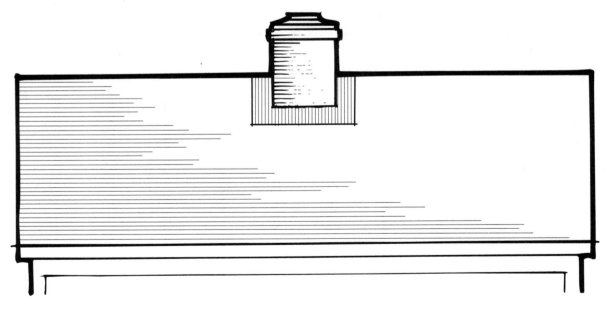

Roof texture can be broken back to simulate sun on roof.
Use the same technique for brickwork.

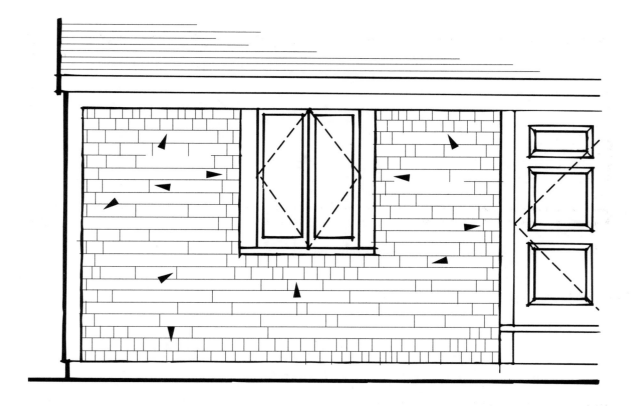

Shingles can be plain horizontal lines, broken back like the roof. As an alternative, use continuous horizontal lines with vertical shingle lines. Accent the corners, windows, doors, eaves, and the bottom course of shingles by using more vertical lines at these areas. Use a triangle against a parallel straightedge to do this. Spot a few vertical lines in the empty spaces.

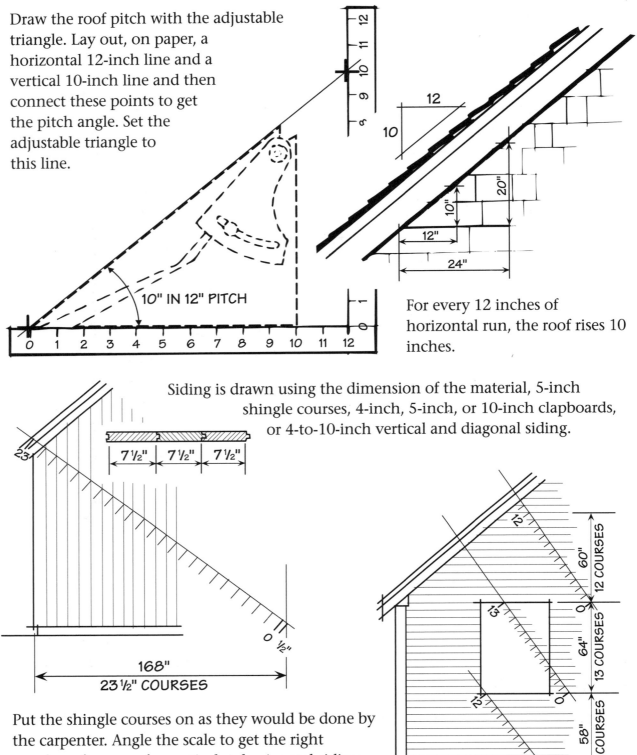

Draw the roof pitch with the adjustable triangle. Lay out, on paper, a horizontal 12-inch line and a vertical 10-inch line and then connect these points to get the pitch angle. Set the adjustable triangle to this line.

10" IN 12" PITCH

For every 12 inches of horizontal run, the roof rises 10 inches.

Siding is drawn using the dimension of the material, 5-inch shingle courses, 4-inch, 5-inch, or 10-inch clapboards, or 4-to-10-inch vertical and diagonal siding.

168"
23½" COURSES

Put the shingle courses on as they would be done by the carpenter. Angle the scale to get the right number of courses for vertical or horizontal siding.

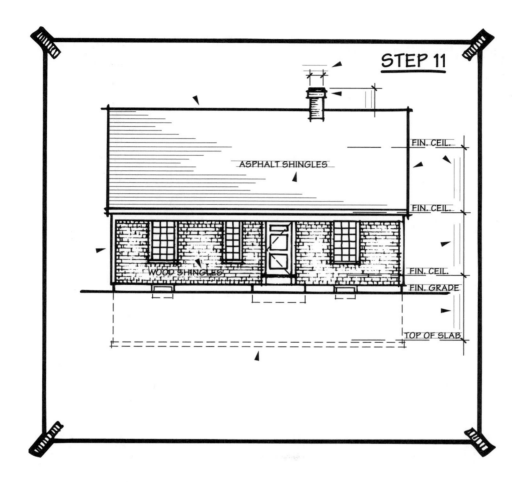

This is a good drawing to show the relationship between the foundation and the finished grade. Dimension the floor heights and chimney size. Heavy up the whole drawing and, in particular, the finish grade and the outline of the house.

The main steps, 1 through 11, are followed by the details. There should be at least one section through the building showing foundation, exterior wall, and roof.

⊜ Drafting

Details can be drawn at any time. Make sketches of them as you go along. These details will make things easier for the builder and show the building inspector how the house is to be built. He can tell you before it's built if it is acceptable.

When drawing details, punch up the sections that the drawing cuts through—things like 2x4 plates, joists, trim, and foundation.

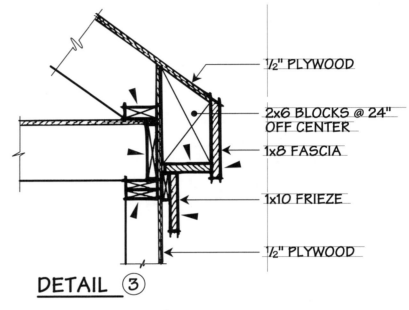

½" PLYWOOD

2x6 BLOCKS @ 24" OFF CENTER

1x8 FASCIA

1x10 FRIEZE

½" PLYWOOD

DETAIL ③

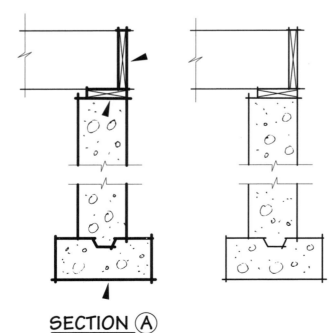

SECTION Ⓐ

Draw all the details that fit on a sheet before lettering. The procedure is similar to drawing floor plans: light layout, then heavier for clarity, dimension lines, lettering, final punching up of the line work, and last the heavy line.

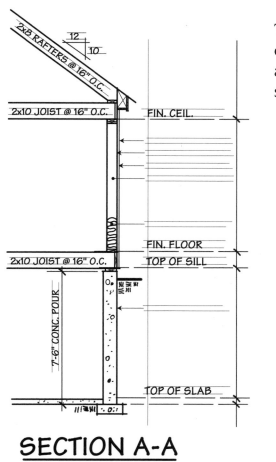

2x8 RAFTERS @ 16" O.C.

12
10

2x10 JOIST @ 16" O.C.   FIN. CEIL.

FIN. FLOOR

2x10 JOIST @ 16" O.C.   TOP OF SILL

7'-6" CONC. POUR

TOP OF SLAB

SECTION A-A

The section through the building is really a large detail at ⅜-inch scale. You can't show much detail at a scale smaller than that; but if the section is simple, then ¼-inch scale will work.

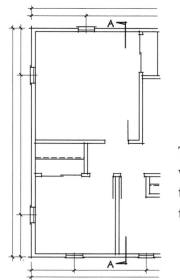

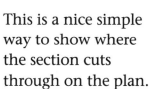

A

This is a nice simple way to show where the section cuts through on the plan.

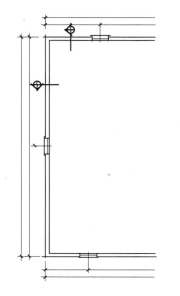

F
3
SECTION LETTER
SHEET SECTION IS ON

This system is good if there are a lot of drawings. It makes it easy to locate a specific detail or section. The top letter is the section letter and the bottom number is the sheet the section is on.

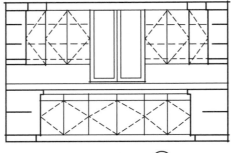

ELEVATION ①

Interior room elevations are useful, particularly in the kitchen and fireplace wall. You can show exactly what is to be built there. A ¼-inch scale is usual, but a larger size is used when more detail is required.

The system for showing the location on the plan is a circle-arrow combination. The top number is the elevation number and the bottom one is the sheet the elevation is on.

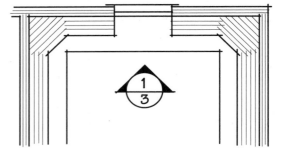

ELEVATION NUMBER
SHEET ELEVATION IS ON

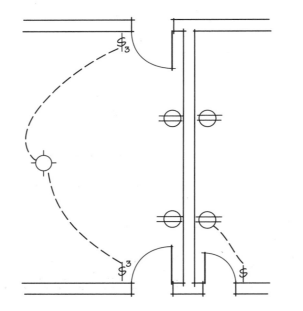

LIGHT — CEILING

LIGHT — WALL

LIGHT — PULL CHAIN

CONVENIENCE OUTLET

RANGE OUTLET

WATER-PROOF OUTLET

SWITCH

3-WAY SWITCH

The electric plan is simple and usually put on the floor plans. If the plans are very "busy," a separate floor plan can be traced and the electrical layout drawn on it.

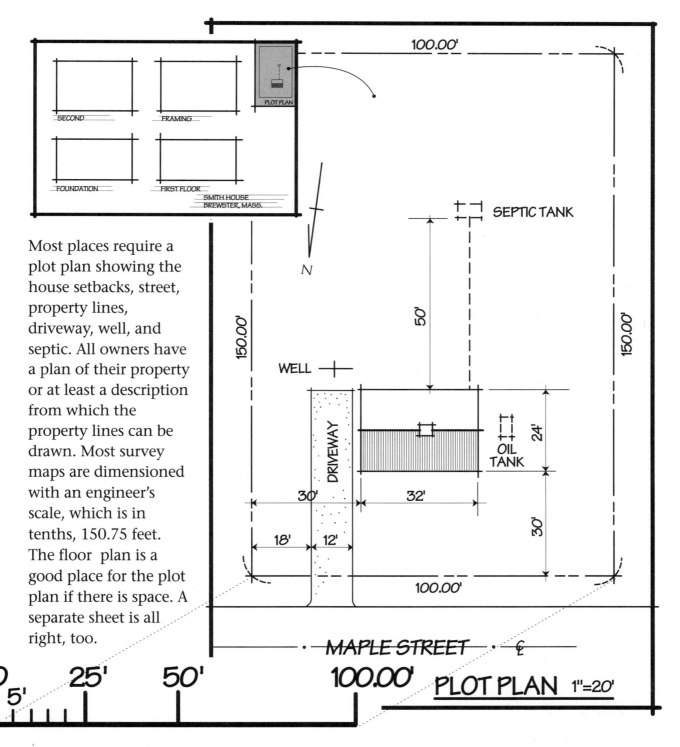

Most places require a plot plan showing the house setbacks, street, property lines, driveway, well, and septic. All owners have a plan of their property or at least a description from which the property lines can be drawn. Most survey maps are dimensioned with an engineer's scale, which is in tenths, 150.75 feet. The floor plan is a good place for the plot plan if there is space. A separate sheet is all right, too.

PLOT PLAN 1"=20'

If an engineer's scale is not available, make a scale using your survey plan. Divide up some dimension until you get what you need. Draw the plot plan at whatever scale is convenient.

DOOR SCHEDULE

MARK	SIZE	MATERIALS	PATTERN	REMARKS
Ⓐ	3'-0" x 6'-8" x 1¾"	FIR	108 (F-66-2)	
Ⓑ	2'-6" x 6'-8" x 1¾"	FIR	L (F-944)	
Ⓒ	2'-6" x 6'-6" x 1⅜"	PINE	M-1051	
Ⓓ	2'-4" x 6'-6" x 1⅜"	PINE	M-1051	
Ⓔ				

The door schedule leaves no doubt as to what is required. It's pretty tough to fit all that information on the plan.

With the door schedule the symbol is shown on the plan.

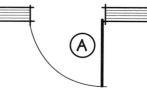

With no schedule, the size is shown on the plan.

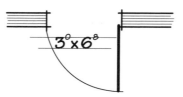

Here is another way to show a door.

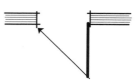

WINDOW SCHEDULE

MARK	UNIT NO.	AMOUNT REQ.
⟨1⟩	3446	3
⟨2⟩	2042	1
⟨3⟩	C-235	1

The window schedule works like the door schedule.

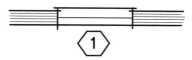

With the schedule, the symbol is shown on the plan.

With no schedule, the unit number is shown.

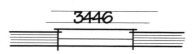

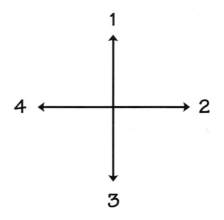

ROOM FINISH

ROOM	FLOOR	WALLS	CEILING	BASE	TRIM	REMARKS
ENTRANCE	Vinyl Sheet	½"Sheetrock	½"Sheetrock	Rubber	Pine	
LIVINGROOM	White Oak	½"Sheetrock	½"Sheetrock	1 x 5	Pine	
DININGROOM	White Oak	½"Sheetrock	½"Sheetrock	1 x 5	Pine	
KITCHEN	Vinyl Sheet	½"Sheetrock	½"Sheetrock	Rubber	Pine	
BATH #1	Vinyl Sheet	½"Sheetrock	½"Sheetrock	Rubber	Pine	ceramic tile in tub.

To avoid surprising the builder, a room finish schedule is a great help.

Some jobs might require identifying each wall in a room because of many different finishes. This can be done with this symbol on every floor plan. Any place will do.

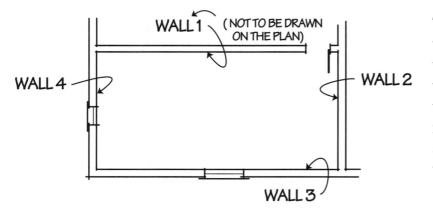

The room finish schedule with this system will show wall 1, wall 2, wall 3, and wall 4. The number 1 wall will always be the upper, number 2 the right, number 3 the bottom, and number 4 the left.

The lead for lettering should be soft and dark, either F or HB. The point, before sharpening, looks like this. Not until the tip is sharpened by sandpaper or sharpener is it ready to work with.

To get thin vertical lines, roll the pencil to a sharp corner on the tip and then stroke. Find the broad part of the tip for the horizontal and curved strokes. This combination makes for clean, crisp lettering.

Experiment with the tip; you might like the chisel point, which is used the same way: thin vertical stroke and broad horizontal stroke. Make all strokes from the shoulder, not the wrist. Use firm, sure vertical strokes and quick, smooth curves. There is a lot of lettering on a plan, and speed is a great help in getting a job done. But above all, it must be clear. If you can't read it, the pretty art is worthless. Practice and develop your own style. Hold the pencil with a light touch and you will have better control.

The titles are put on all the sheets when the plans are done.

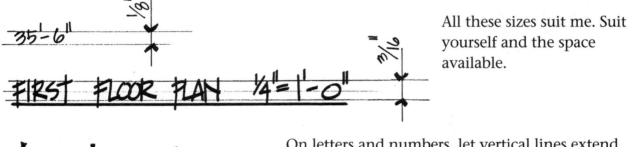

All these sizes suit me. Suit yourself and the space available.

On letters and numbers, let vertical lines extend beyond guide lines. Make horizontal and curves ride up. Some letters can run together.

You get a hangdog look when vertical lines slant and horizontal lines drop.

Quick, firm vertical strokes

Quick, smooth curves

Let the guidelines show on the prints. I think they help the looks of the lettering. Keep them thin so they don't conflict with dimension lines.

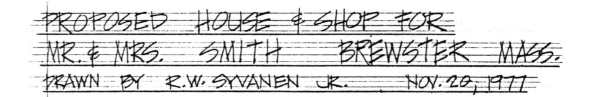

This is my style for fast lettering. I used three lines.

You can do the same thing on two lines.

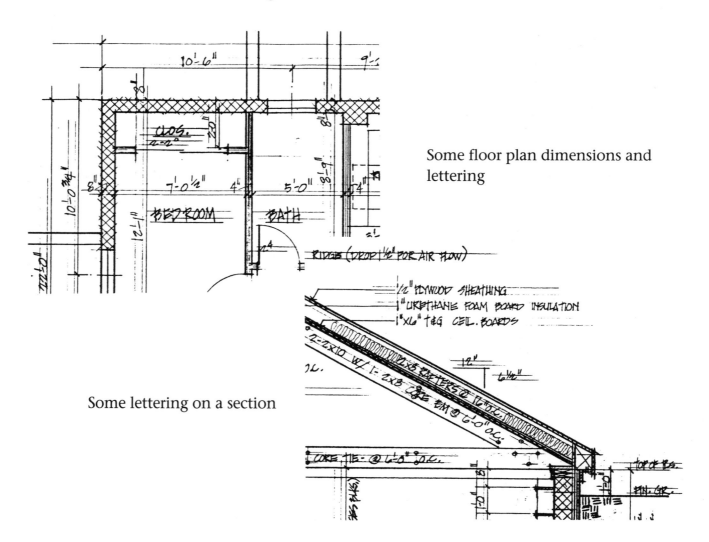

Some floor plan dimensions and lettering

Some lettering on a section

These are the most common symbols:

 Wood blocking

Wood timber

Finish wood or trim

Plywood

Concrete block

Poured concrete

Sand

Fiberglass insulation

Rigid insulation

Foam board

Brick (section)

⬤ Drafting

———————/———————. Broken line or section

——— · ——— · ₵——— Center line

— — — — — — — — — Buried or hidden line

▬▬ ▬ ▬▬ ▬ ▬▬ ▬ Beam

———————————— Guidelines

———————————— Dimension lines

▬▬▬▬▬▬▬▬▬▬ Heavy outline

FINISHED GRADE Earth

Gravel

ABBREVIATIONS

These abbreviations are always used. Try to spell all other words for clarity.

O.C. = ON CENTER — 16" O.C.   **₵** = CENTER LINE — ——·₵·——

& = AND — SAND & GRAVEL   **w/** = WITH — ½" w/PLYWOOD OVER

@ = AT — 2x4 STUDS @ 16" O.C.   **CONC.** = CONCRETE

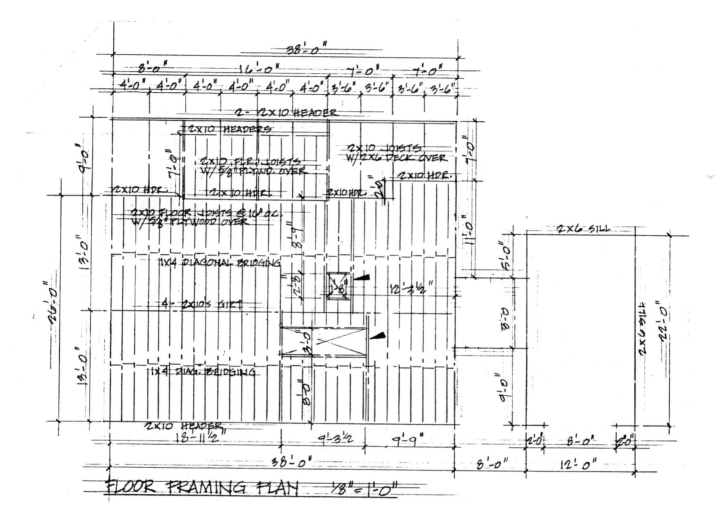

FLOOR FRAMING PLAN ⅛"=1'-0"

Floor framing plans can be drawm at any scale from ⅟₁₆" = 1'-0" to ¼" = 1'-0". This plan worked well for me at ⅛" = 1'-0". Where chimney and stairs are, "X" them to show there is no framing.

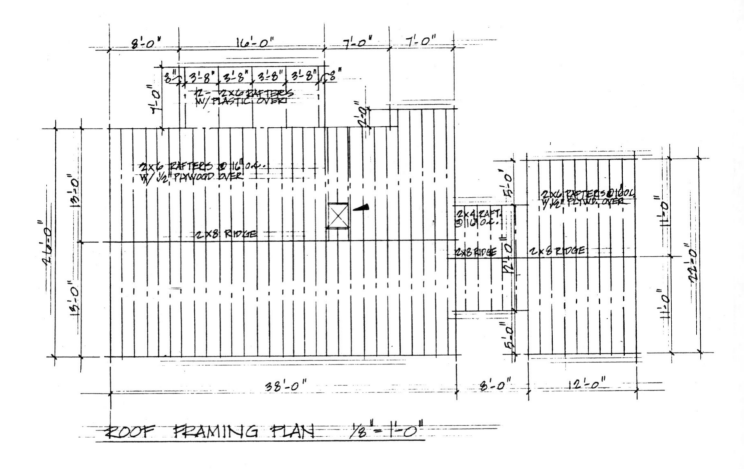

ROOF FRAMING PLAN   1/8"=1'-0"

This roof framing plan is from the same set of plans. Again, "X" where there is an opening. In this case it is the chimney.

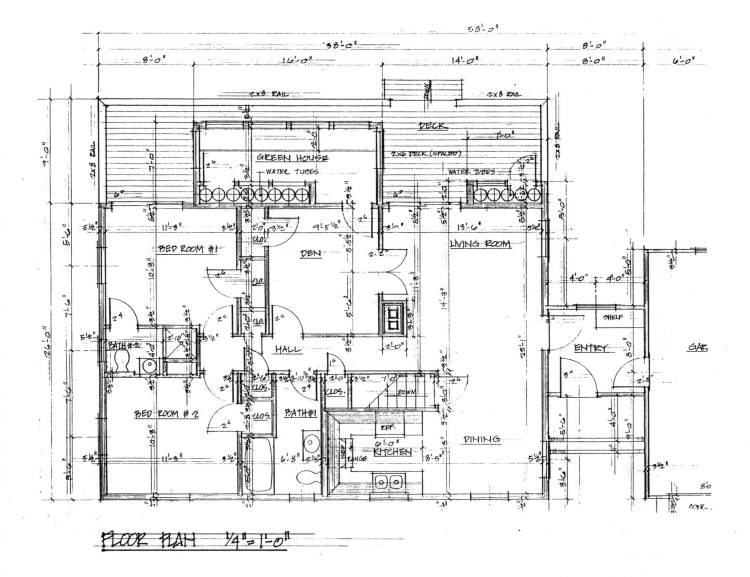

FLOOR PLAN   ¼" = 1'-0"

This floor plan is typical. It shows all that is necessary for construction. The roof and floor framing plans are from this plan.

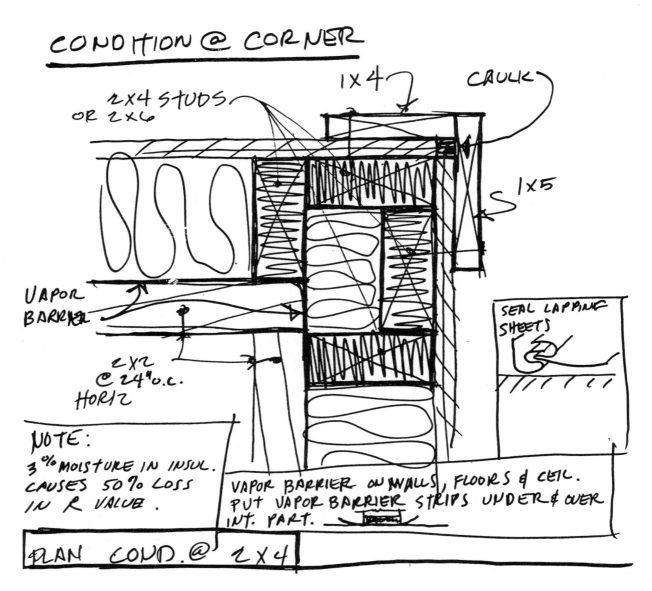

CONDITION @ CORNER

2X4 STUDS
OR 2X6

1X4

CAULK

1X5

VAPOR BARRIER

2X2 @ 24" O.C. HORIZ

SEAL LAPPING SHEETS

NOTE:
3% MOISTURE IN INSUL.
CAUSES 50% LOSS
IN R VALUE.

VAPOR BARRIER ON WALLS, FLOORS & CEIL.
PUT VAPOR BARRIER STRIPS UNDER & OVER
INT. PART.

PLAN COND. @ 2X4

Details can be as simple as this to get the job done. This is what the carpenter does on the job if the details are not on the plans. If you want the job done your way, it is best to draw it first. This is a plan of an outside corner for a Scandinavian wall. There is good nailing for the corner boards and access to insulate the corner from inside the building. This makes a nice tight draft-free corner.

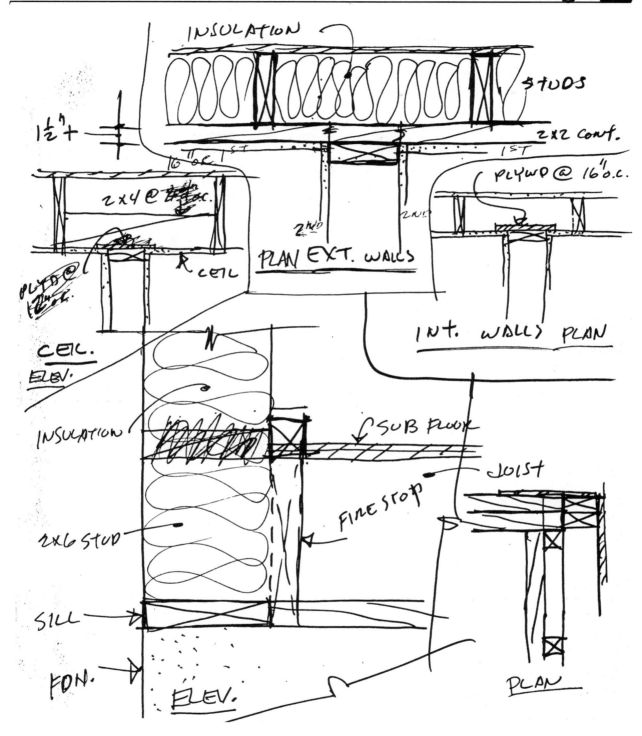

INSULATION

STUDS

$1\frac{1}{2}"+$

16" o.c.   1ST

2X4 @ 16" o.c.

PLYWD@ Fl o.c.

CEIL.

2X2 cont.

1ST

PLYWD @ 16" o.c.

2ND   2ND

PLAN EXT. WALLS

INT. WALLS PLAN

CEIL.
ELEV.

INSULATION

SUB FLOOR

JOIST

FIRESTOP

2X6 STUD

SILL

FDN.

ELEV.

PLAN

More quick sketch details that work but are not always clear to others. Use felt-tip pen or soft pencil.

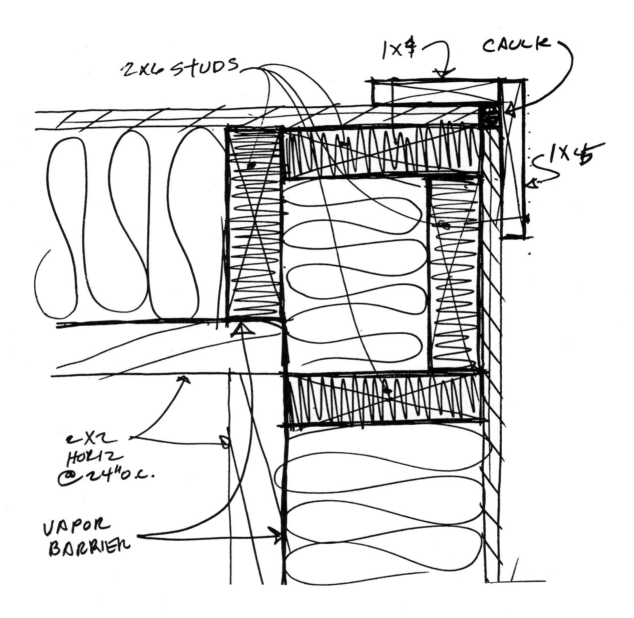

2X6 STUDS

1X4   CAULK

1X5

2X2 HORIZ @24"O.C.

VAPOR BARRIER

The same Scandinavian-wall detail with 2x6 studs. All these quick sketch details can be used as is and photocopies made to pass around.

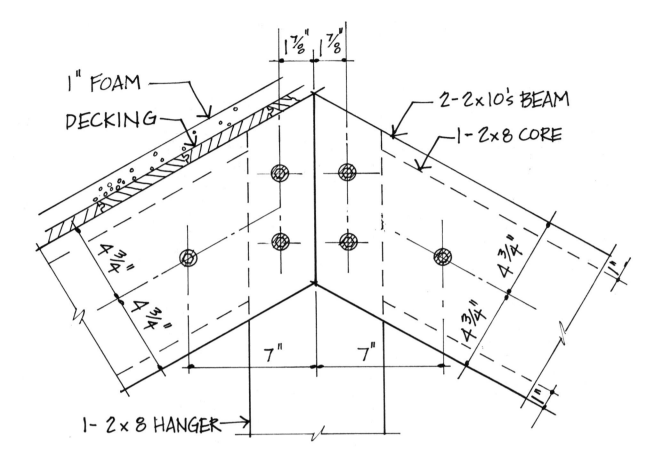

1" FOAM

DECKING

1 7/8" 7/8"

2-2x10's BEAM

1-2x8 CORE

4 3/4"

4 3/4"

4 3/4"

4 3/4"

7"   7"

4 3/4"

1- 2 x 8 HANGER →

BEAM & HANGER @ RIDGE
3" = 1'-0"

10/13

When a little more precision is required, I go to this system. At this scale, things can be measured off easily.

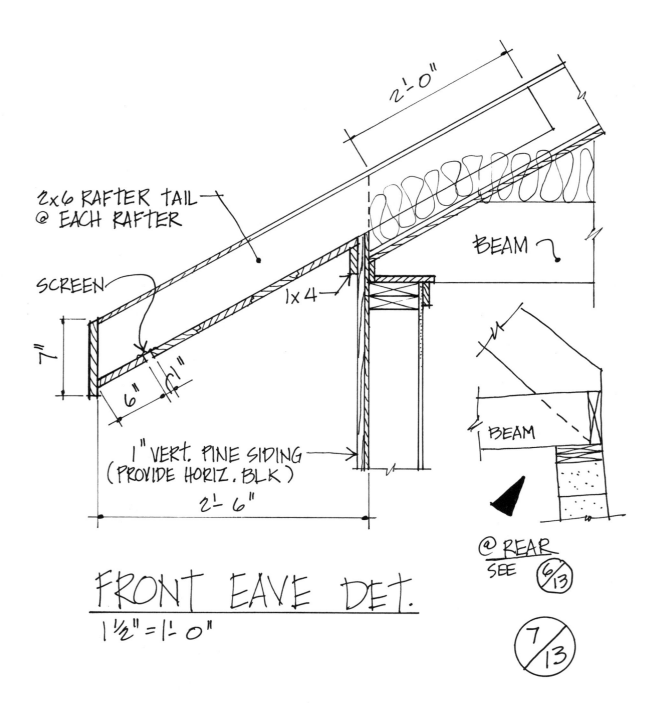

2x6 RAFTER TAIL @ EACH RAFTER

SCREEN

7"

2'-0"

BEAM

1x4

6" 1"

1" VERT. PINE SIDING (PROVIDE HORIZ. BLK)

2'-6"

FRONT EAVE DET.
1½" = 1'-0"

BEAM

@ REAR
SEE 6/13

7/13

What is drawn doesn't always work best, and a revision takes place in the field.

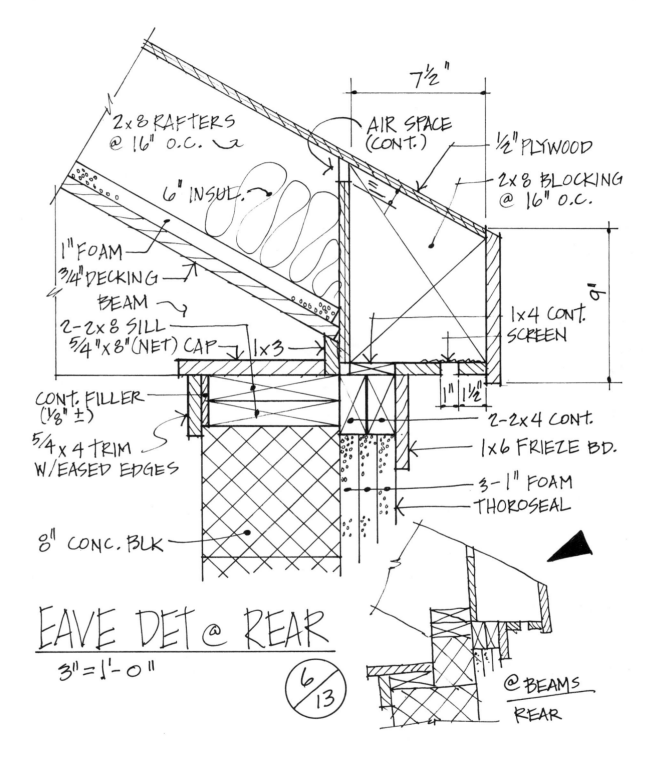

2x8 RAFTERS @ 16" O.C.

6" INSUL.

1" FOAM
3/4" DECKING
BEAM
2-2x8 SILL
5/4"x8"(NET) CAP

1x3

CONT. FILLER (1/8" ±)

5/4 x 4 TRIM W/EASED EDGES

8" CONC. BLK

7½"

AIR SPACE (CONT.)

½" PLYWOOD
2x8 BLOCKING @ 16" O.C.

9"

1x4 CONT. SCREEN

1" 1½"

2-2x4 CONT.
1x6 FRIEZE BD.
3-1" FOAM
THOROSEAL

EAVE DET @ REAR
3" = 1'-0"

6/13

@ BEAMS
REAR

Once again you think you have it all figured, but at least there is a place to start from.

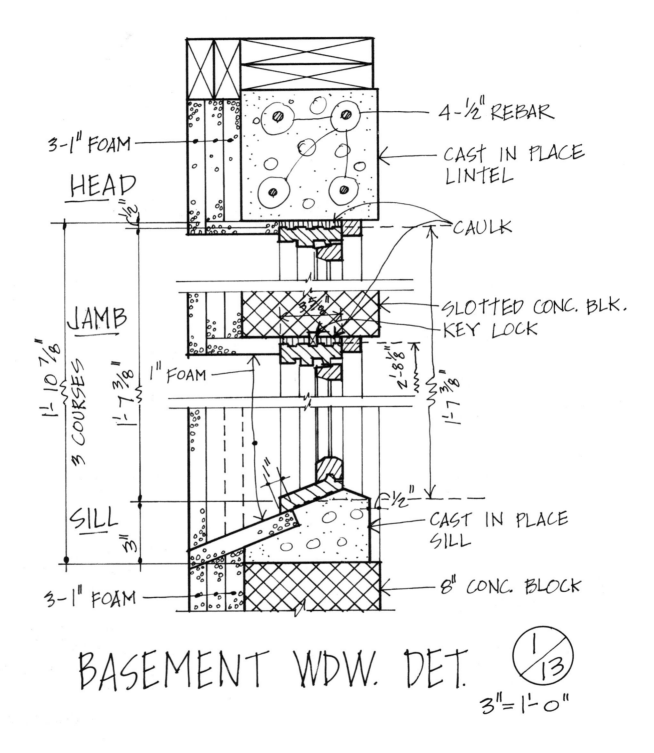

BASEMENT WDW. DET. ①/13

3" = 1'-0"

All these details were drawn on 8½ by 11-inch sheets, in pencil, and photocopies made for use on the job.

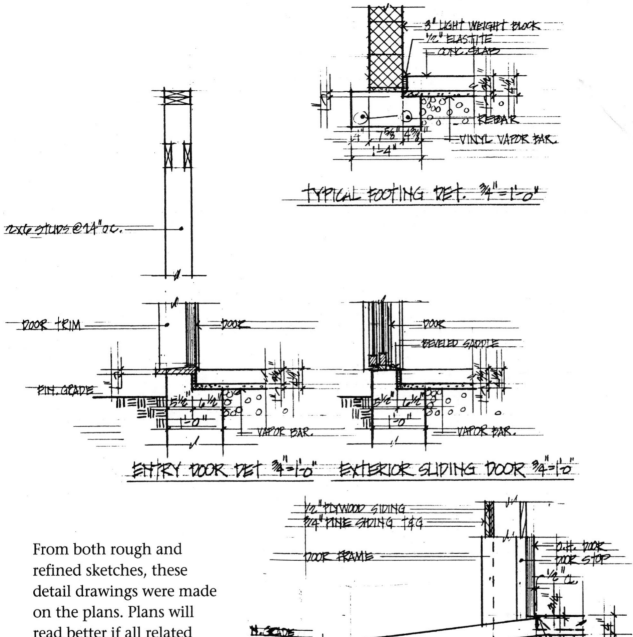

3" LIGHT WEIGHT BLOCK
½" ELASTITE
CONC. SLAB
REBAR
VINYL VAPOR BAR.

7⅝" 4⅞"
1'-4"

TYPICAL FOOTING DET. ¾"=1'-0"

2x6 STUDS @ 14" O.C.

DOOR TRIM
DOOR
FIN. GRADE

5½" 6½"
1'-0"
VAPOR BAR.

ENTRY DOOR DET ¾"=1'-0"

DOOR
BEVELED SADDLE

5½" 6½"
1'-0"
VAPOR BAR.

EXTERIOR SLIDING DOOR ¾"=1'-0"

From both rough and refined sketches, these detail drawings were made on the plans. Plans will read better if all related details, like foundation details or window details, are kept together.

½" PLYWOOD SIDING
¾" PINE SIDING T&G
DOOR FRAME

FIN. GRADE

EXT. DOOR
DOOR STOP
½"

2"x2"x¼"

9¼"

6" COMPACTED GRAVEL

8"

CONCRETE APRON DETAIL ¾"=1'-0"

Perspectives can be a great help in visualizing the finished product. They can be plain or fancy. There is a lot written on this subject, and, in fact, most architectural firms farm this work out.

You might try simple work like this that I did for a remodel job.

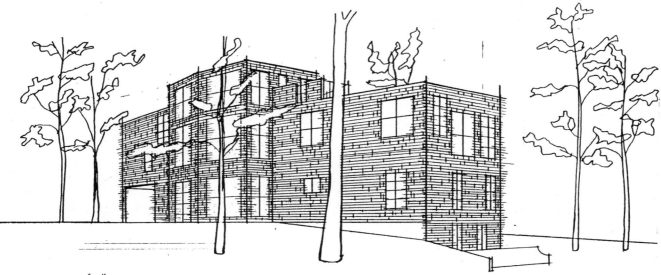

ELEVATION "A"   WHITE CEDAR SHINGLES SIDING

I used simple perspective techniques, the old "vanishing points" many of us learned about in high school.

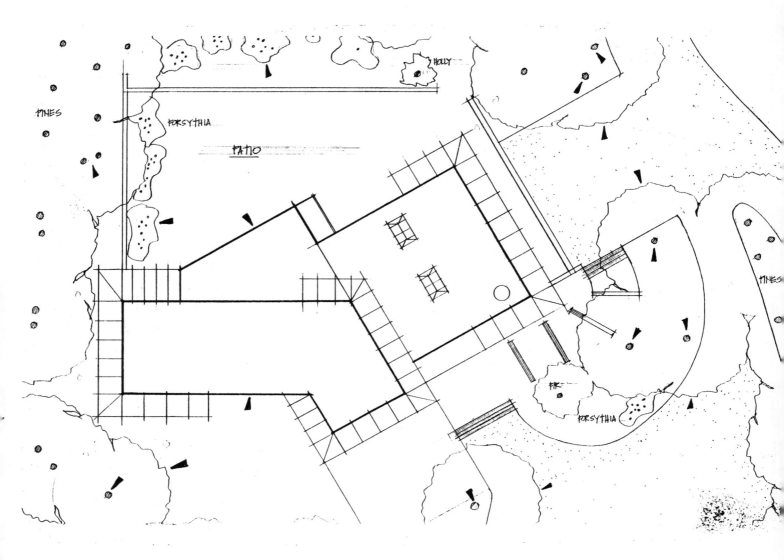

This landscape plan shows the roof and surrounding foliage. The tree trunks are located, and then the shapes are simulated around them.

A small house is usually easy to draw but not always easy to design. With a large house there is ample space to work with—stairways, kitchen appliances, tubs, and sinks will fit anywhere. A small house is limiting; clever design is necessary.

The following pages show a small passive, solar house that worked well. As with any house, the owners made changes they wish they hadn't and thought too late of things they should have done. I don't know of anyone who has built the "perfect house." There are always things that "should" have been done differently.

Skylights are great; but they have a tendency to leak, are difficult to shade in summer, and lose much heat in winter. A well-built skylight, properly installed, should not leak. Mother Nature, with a tall leafy tree, or any other well-designed sun screen, will take care of the summer sun. Insulating panels or drapes (the simpler the better) will keep the winter heat in.

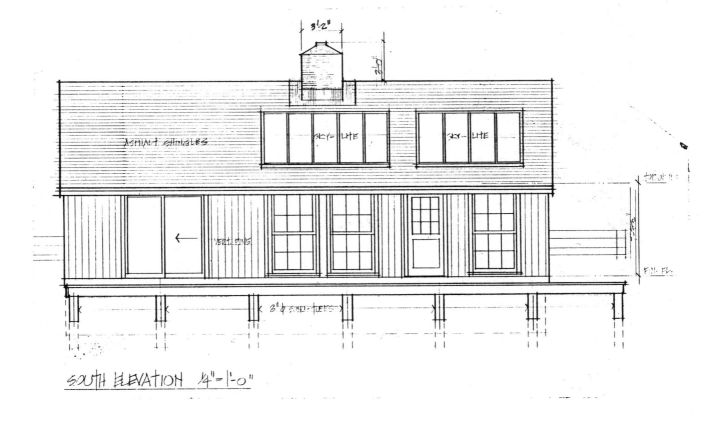

SOUTH ELEVATION 1/4"=1'-0"

They don't always turn out the same as the plans.

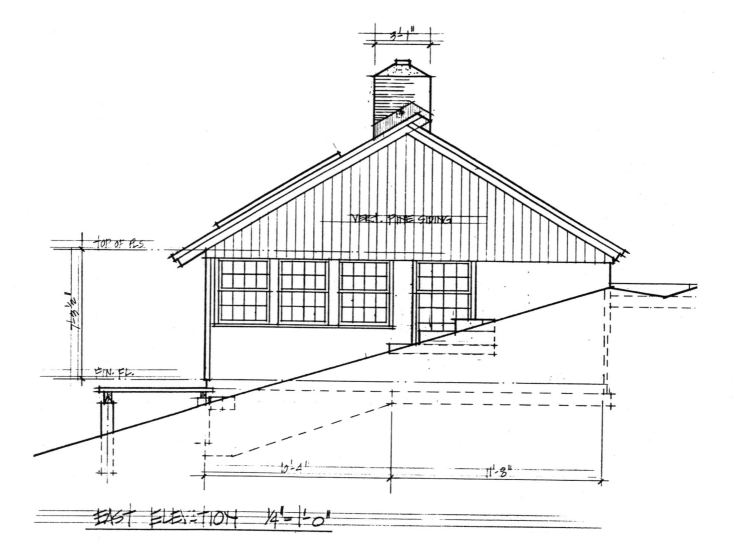

EAST ELEVATION ¼"=1'-0"

This house wasn't built on the original location, and that's why there is a difference in ground slope. It worked better this way.

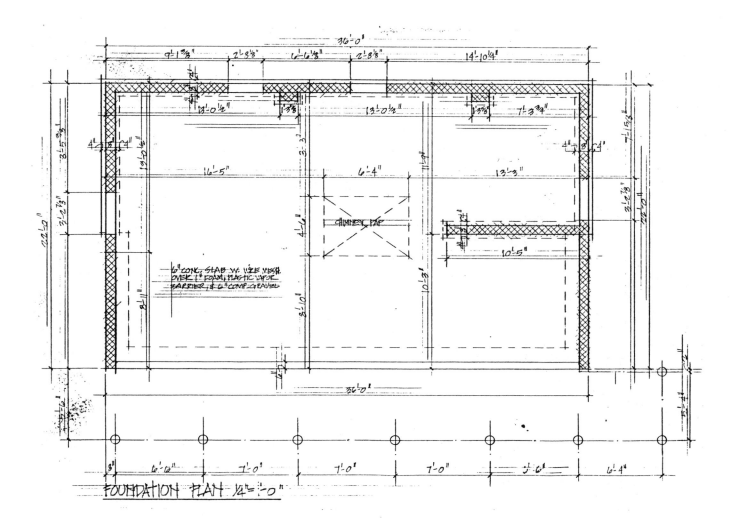

FOUNDATION PLAN ¼"=1'-0"

The foundation was to be concrete block, but poured concrete was used to save time.

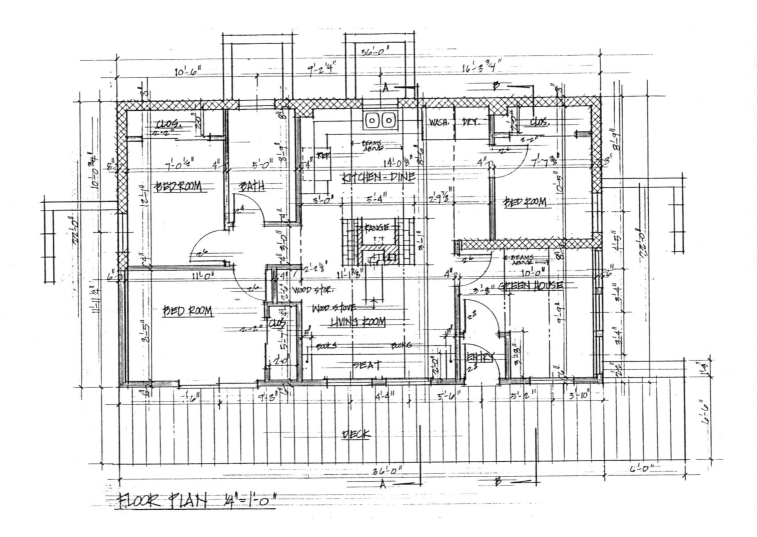

FLOOR PLAN ¼"=1'-0"

It was a simple floor plan that was easy to draw. The air-lock entry was not built; the owners wish it had been.

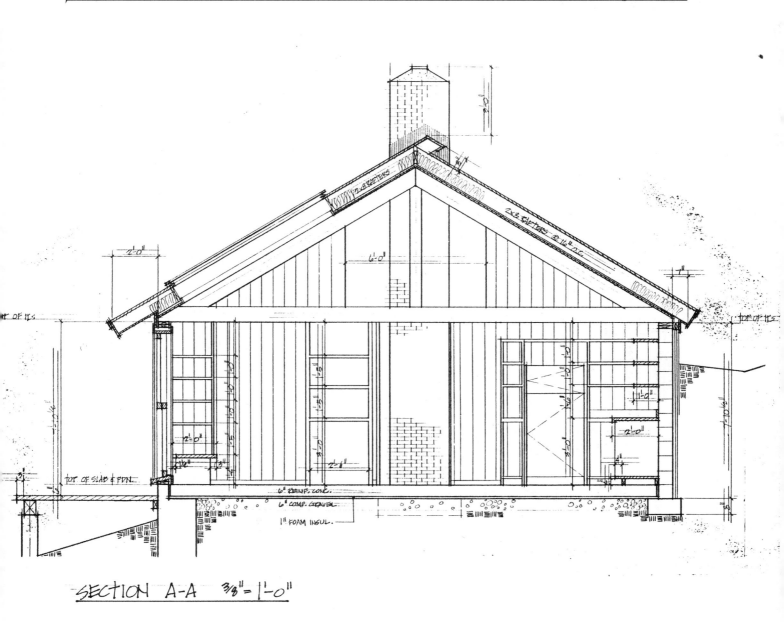

SECTION A-A   3/8"= 1'-0"

A section through the building showing all that you would see if looking in that direction. The floor plan shows where it cuts through. The foam insulation under the concrete-slab floor should be under the gravel and on top of a vapor barrier. The gravel would then store heat along with the floor slab.

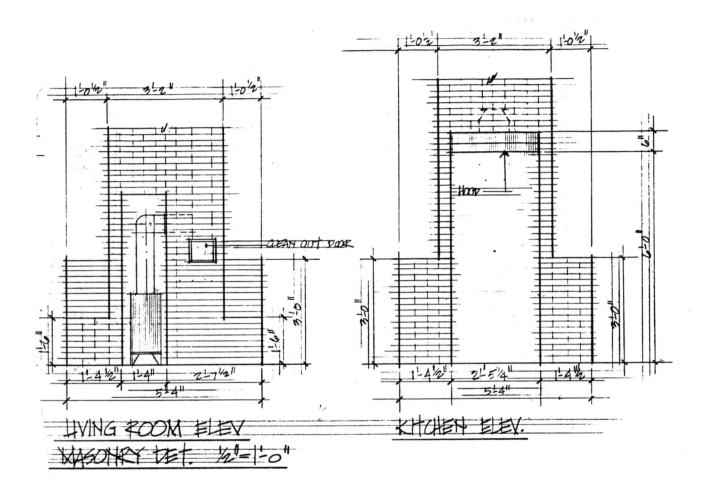

LIVING ROOM ELEV

MASONRY DET. ½"=1'-0"

KITCHEN ELEV.

This masonry unit was not built, either. The owners opted for a fireplace, which turned out very nice. Fireplaces are not very energy efficient, but they can be good heat radiators if the Rumford style is used. The Rumford-style opening is wide and high (about as high as it is wide), with a shallow hearth. There is a good paperback book about this fireplace, *The Forgotten Art of Building a Good Fireplace,* written by Vrest Orton and published by Yankee Books in 1969.

Most small houses are low-budget houses, which adds to the design difficulty. The following house-shop design was no exception.

The owners wanted three things: a shop with an old look, passive-solar living quarters, and a warm look in the concrete living quarters. The old look is accomplished with unpainted pine siding. There is a lot of glass on the south, two Trombe walls, and a greenhouse, all of which give this house tremendous heating potential. The living room, dining, and kitchen area has 4x6 adzed beams with a wood ceiling to give it a warm look.

The porch on the shop entrance side is inviting.

The skylight needs shading.

This is an example of a simple, quick perspective; and because I built the house, the finished product is pretty much the same.

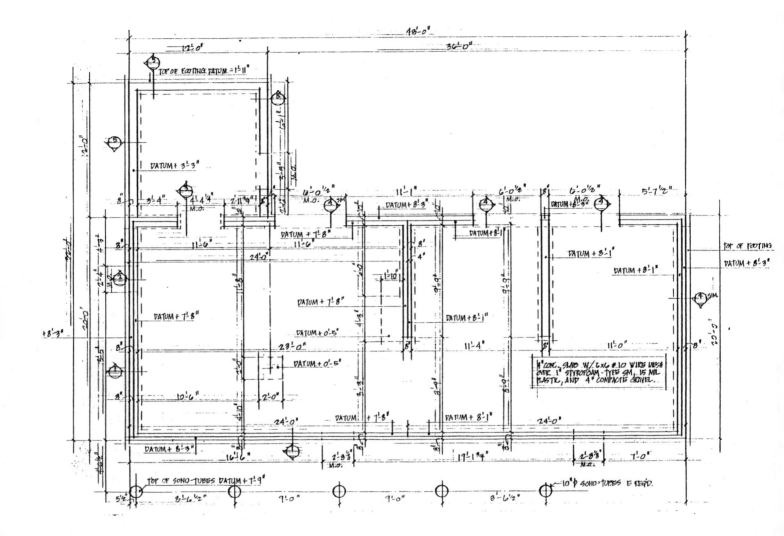

I had a lot of different concrete heights, so I called them out as datum +8'=1" or datum +8'=3". The concrete contractor found it too much trouble, so I made some changes. The simpler the plans are, the fewer problems you will encounter.

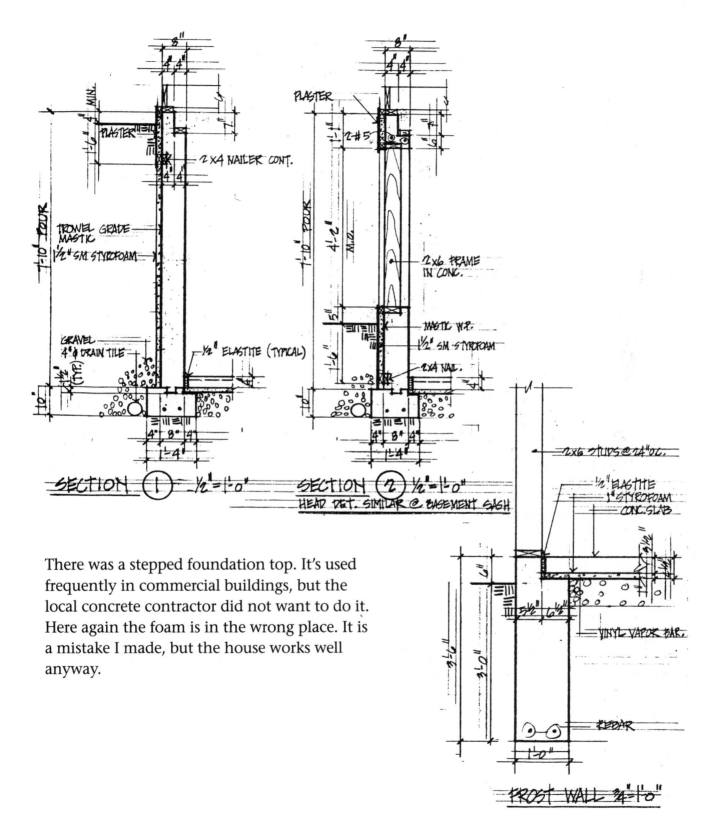

SECTION ① ½"=1'-0"

SECTION ② ½"=1'-0"
HEAD DET. SIMILAR @ BASEMENT SASH

FROST WALL ¾"=1'-0"

There was a stepped foundation top. It's used frequently in commercial buildings, but the local concrete contractor did not want to do it. Here again the foam is in the wrong place. It is a mistake I made, but the house works well anyway.

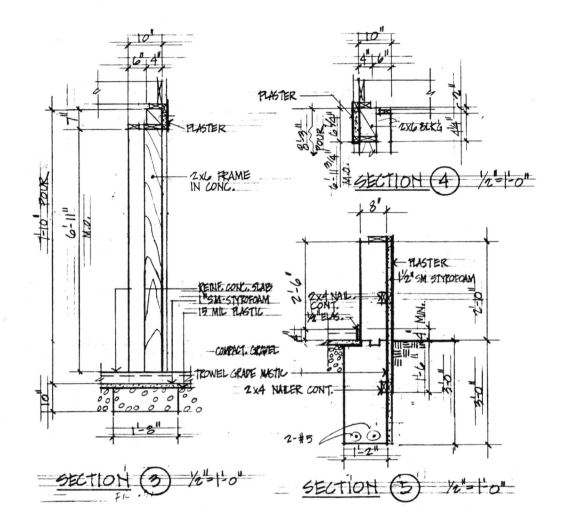

These details were drawn on the sheet with the foundation plans; they're easier to read that way. As you look around, you will find many ways to do the same job, and just because it hasn't been done that way before doesn't mean it's wrong.

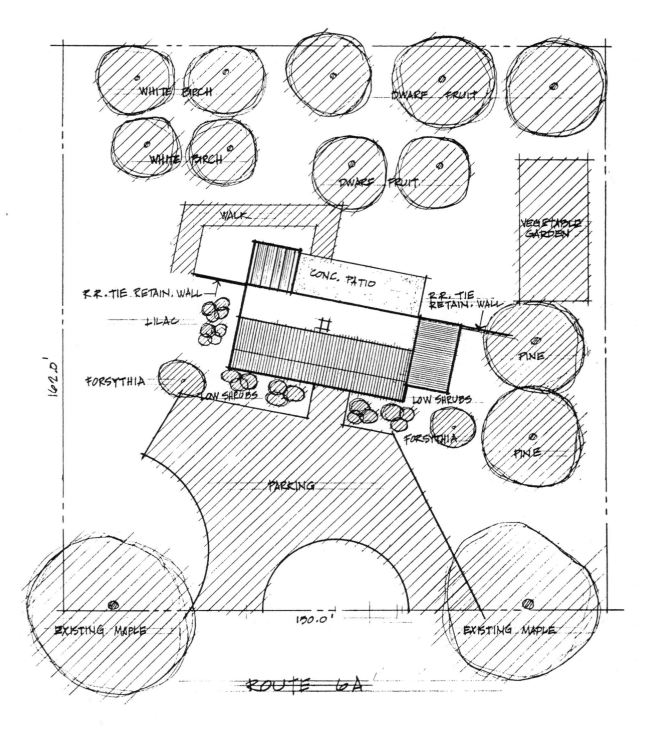

Another example of a landscape plot plan. This plan was done because of a local regulation. That's what they wanted, so that's what we gave them.

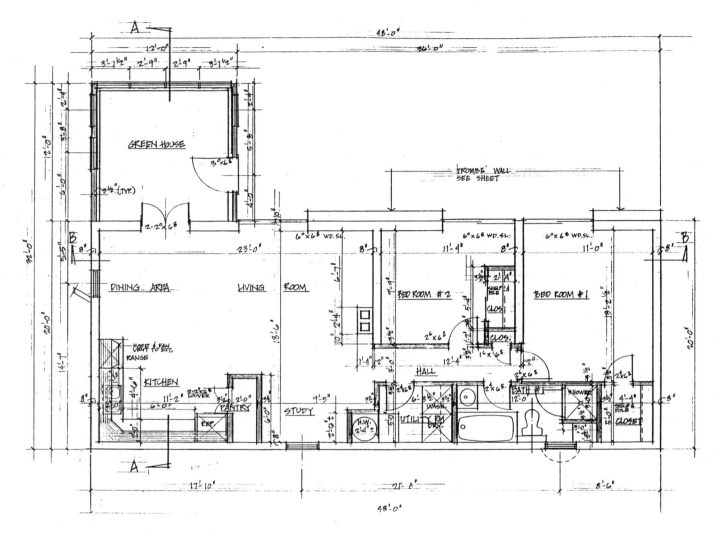

FLOOR PLAN   1/4" = 1'-0"

Another simple floor plan. I have found that the easier it is to draw, the easier it is to build.

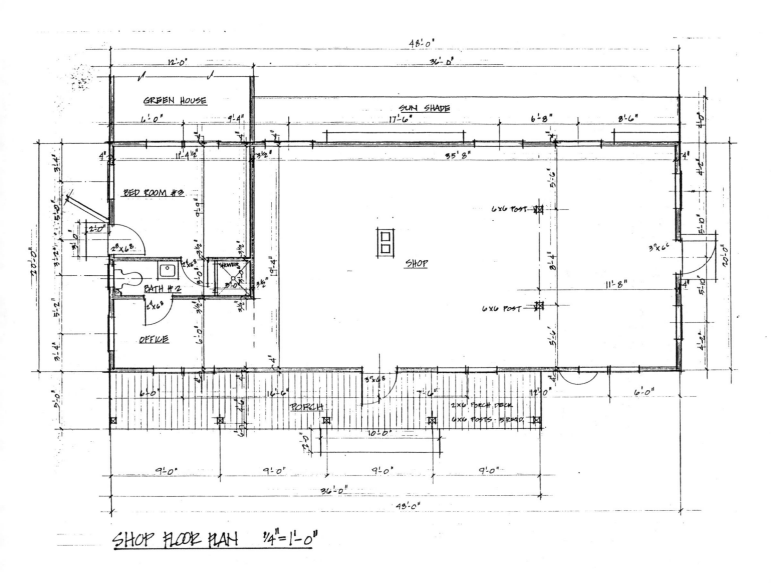

SHOP FLOOR PLAN ¼"=1'-0"

I cut off part of the greenhouse on this drawing because it did not fit on the sheet. It was unnecessary to draw it all here anyway, because it is on the previous sheet (see page 100).

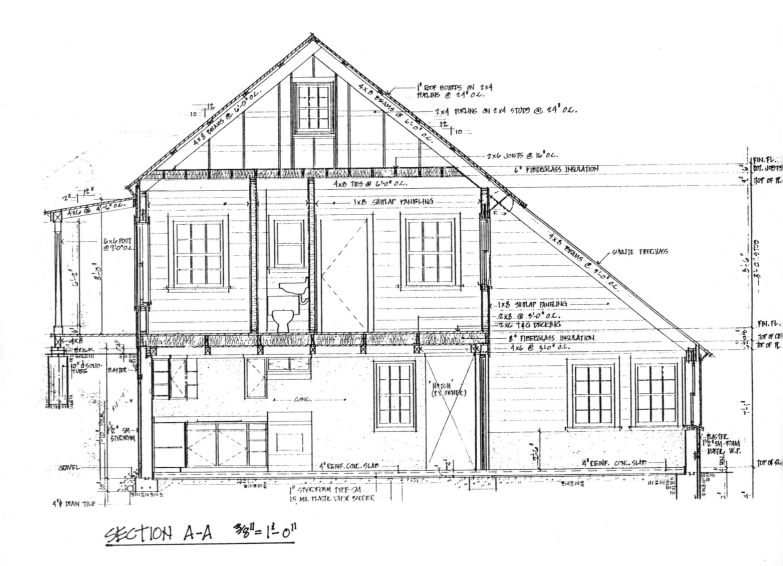

SECTION A-A   3/8" = 1'-0"

Here's a section through the main house and greenhouse. The foam insulation is wrong here, too.

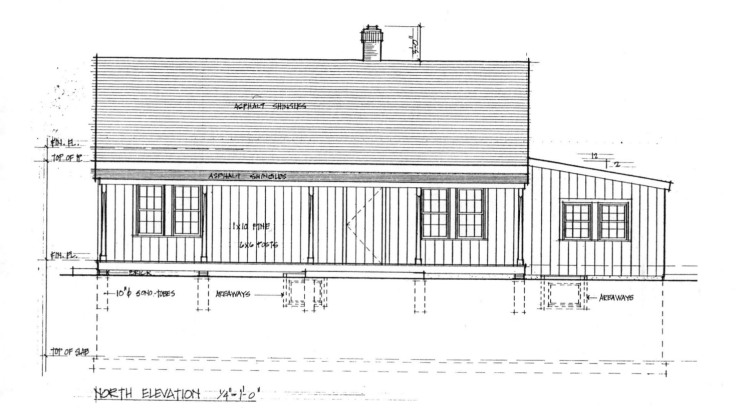

NORTH ELEVATION ¼"=1'-0"

This is a very simple building with very simple elevations.

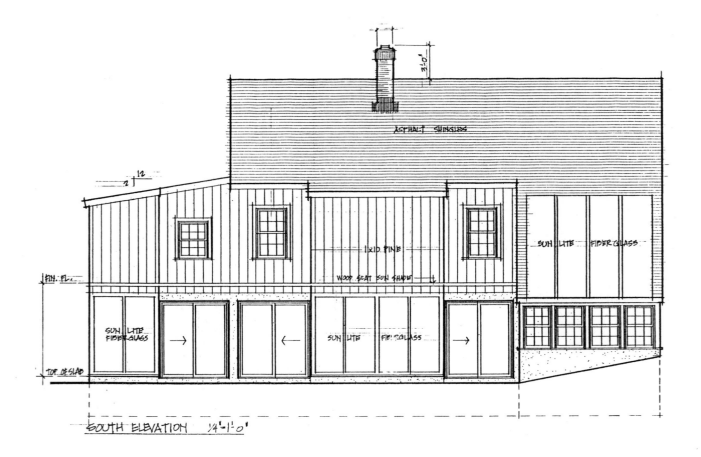

ASPHALT SHINGLES

1x10 PINE

WOOD SLAT SUN SHADE

SUN LITE FIBER GLASS

SUN LITE FIBERGLASS

SUN LITE FIBERGLASS

FIN. FL.

TOP OF SLAB

SOUTH ELEVATION ¼"=1'-0"

It's a little more complicated on the south side.

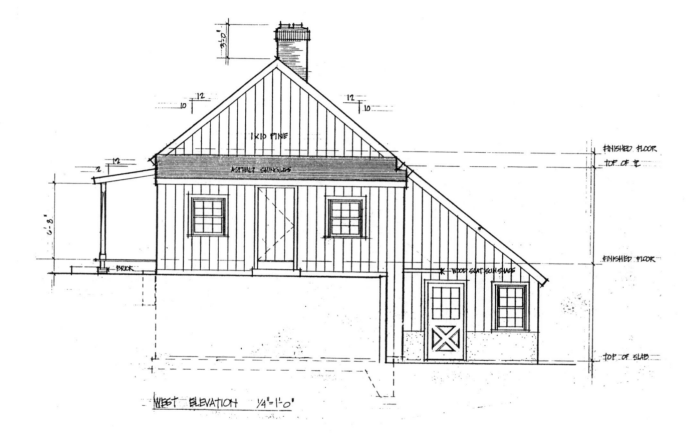

WEST ELEVATION ¼"=1'-0"

This elevation shows up the different ground levels as well as the foundation conditions.